Sacred Spaces

Transforming Your Life and Home for Positive Energy

Elo Marc

Introduction

This book guides readers through techniques to eliminate bad vibes from their living space and personal life. It combines ancient wisdom, modern psychology, and actionable steps to create a sanctuary of peace and positivity.

Elo Marc

Chapter 1

The Power of Energy in Your Space and Life

Your surroundings play a profound role in shaping your emotional and mental well-being. Every object, corner, and interaction in your home holds energy, which can either uplift or drain you. By becoming aware of the energetic imprints in your environment and life, you gain the power to transform them, fostering harmony and vitality.

Why Energy Matters

Energy isn't just an abstract concept—it's tangible in the way clutter feels suffocating, a vibrant home feels inviting, or certain people leave you refreshed or drained. This energetic resonance stems from ancient philosophies like Feng Shui and Vastu Shastra, which emphasize the interplay between space, objects, and human emotions. Modern psychology echoes these ideas, linking tidy, well-lit, and thoughtfully arranged spaces to increased focus and decreased anxiety.

How Spaces Reflect Inner Energy

The condition of your home mirrors your inner state. A cluttered room might indicate unresolved emotional baggage, while a well-maintained space radiates clarity and purpose. When we align our living spaces with positive energy, they not only nurture us but also amplify our aspirations, serving as a physical and energetic foundation for growth.

The Ripple Effect of Cleansing

Cleansing your space is a gateway to holistic transformation. By purging negativity from your environment, you clear mental pathways, reduce stress, and enhance focus. This act isn't just about removing physical dirt but also about resetting energetic patterns, making space for joy, creativity, and abundance.

Key Takeaways for This Book Section:

• **Impact of Environment on Mood**: Discuss how space design and clutter affect emotional states.

• **Scientific Support**: Introduce studies linking organized, clean environments with mental clarity.

• **Practical Relevance**: Highlight how small energetic shifts in the home can lead to big changes in life.

This introduction sets the stage for the transformative practices detailed in later chapters, inspiring readers to embrace their role as active creators of their energy-filled sanctuaries.

Understanding How Physical and Emotional Clutter Affects Well-Being

The Impact of Physical Clutter

Physical clutter—like piles of laundry, disorganized workspaces, or overfilled closets—can overwhelm the senses, creating a sense of chaos. Research shows that cluttered environments increase levels of the stress hormone cortisol, particularly in women, leading to heightened feelings of anxiety and frustration.

• **Distraction and Decreased Focus**: Clutter competes for your attention, reducing the brain's ability to process information effectively. This can make it harder to focus on tasks or relax in your own space.

• **Emotional Drain**: Unfinished projects and disorder often serve as reminders of unmet goals, leading to feelings of guilt or inadequacy.

• **Sleep Disruption**: Studies have shown that messy bedrooms can negatively affect sleep quality, as the brain struggles to associate the space with rest and relaxation.

The Role of Emotional Clutter

Emotional clutter arises from unresolved feelings, toxic relationships, or mental preoccupations. Like physical clutter, it occupies mental space, hindering clarity and emotional balance.

• **Negative Thought Patterns**: Holding onto past regrets or fears can perpetuate cycles of negativity, preventing personal growth.

• **Relationship Strain**: Emotional baggage can seep into interactions, creating tension and miscommunication with loved ones.

• **Energy Drain**: Carrying unresolved emotions can feel like carrying an invisible weight, sapping energy and enthusiasm for new experiences.

The Link Between the Two

Physical and emotional clutter often go hand-in-hand. For instance, people struggling with emotional challenges may accumulate or neglect clutter as a coping mechanism. Conversely, living in a chaotic space can exacerbate feelings of overwhelm, creating a feedback loop of stress.

Simple Practices for Clearing Clutter

• **Physical Space**: Start small—clear one drawer, desk, or closet at a time. Practice the "one in, one out" rule to avoid accumulation.

• **Emotional Space**: Use journaling, mindfulness practices, or therapy to identify and process unresolved emotions.

By addressing both physical and emotional clutter, you create a cleaner slate for a healthier, more peaceful life.

The Science Behind Environmental Energy and Its Impact on Mental Health

Environmental energy, often shaped by physical surroundings and sensory stimuli, directly influences mental health. Scientific research validates how the spaces we inhabit can shape emotional well-being, cognitive function, and stress levels.

1. Sensory Overload and Stress

Cluttered or disorganized environments lead to sensory overload, where competing visual, auditory, or tactile inputs overwhelm the brain. This heightened sensory activity can elevate cortisol levels, the hormone associated with stress, and reduce cognitive efficiency.

• A study from Princeton University Neuroscience Institute found that clutter impedes the brain's ability to focus and process information effectively.

2. Biophilia and Natural Elements

Exposure to natural elements like plants, sunlight, and fresh air enhances mood and reduces stress. This phenomenon, often called "biophilia," underscores humans' innate connection to nature.

• Research published in *Frontiers in Psychology* revealed that indoor plants significantly decrease stress and improve attention levels.

• Natural light also regulates the circadian rhythm, improving sleep quality and overall mental well-being.

3. The Role of Cleanliness and Organization

Tidy spaces promote a sense of control and accomplishment, which can counteract feelings of helplessness. Conversely, mess and chaos correlate with feelings of anxiety and depression.

• A 2010 study from UCLA's Center on Everyday Lives of Families showed that women with cluttered homes had higher cortisol levels, negatively impacting their mood and energy.

4. Positive Energy and Color Psychology

Colors, lighting, and decor evoke emotional responses. For instance:

• **Warm tones** (e.g., red, orange) can energize and stimulate action.

• **Cool tones** (e.g., blue, green) are associated with relaxation and stress reduction.

Additionally, creating spaces with harmonious layouts, such as those guided by Feng Shui principles, promotes a sense of balance and peace.

5. Social and Emotional Energy

Homes where negative interactions frequently occur can "hold" emotional imprints, creating an atmosphere of tension.

Conversely, spaces filled with positive interactions promote relaxation and joy.

Practical Implications:

• **Declutter regularly** to reduce visual stress and maintain focus.

• **Add nature-inspired elements** like plants or water features to increase positive energy.

• **Be mindful of lighting and color choices** to shape the mood of each room.

• **Engage in regular space-clearing rituals** such as smudging or sound therapy to refresh energetic patterns.

By understanding the science of environmental energy, we can intentionally shape our spaces to support mental clarity, emotional resilience, and overall well-being.

Chapter 2

Decluttering the Physical Space

Decluttering your home is more than just an aesthetic exercise—it's a transformative process that can uplift your mood, increase productivity, and improve mental clarity. By removing unnecessary items and organizing your living space, you create an environment that promotes peace and positive energy.

1. Start with a Clear Goal

• Define why you want to declutter: Is it for more space, less stress, or to create a sanctuary? Clear intentions help maintain motivation.

• Break the task into manageable chunks by tackling one room, area, or category at a time.

2. Use Decluttering Methods That Work for You

Here are some popular strategies for tackling clutter:

• **The KonMari Method (Marie Kondo)**: Focus on items

that "spark joy." Hold each object, and decide whether it adds value or happiness to your life. If not, thank it and let it go.

• **Four-Box Technique**: Use boxes labeled *Keep, Donate, Trash, Recycle*. Go through each area systematically, sorting items into these categories.

• **One-In, One-Out Rule**: For every new item you bring into your home, remove one existing item to maintain balance.

3. Practical Steps to Declutter

• **Closets**: Donate clothes you haven't worn in a year. Sort by season and function for easier access.

• **Kitchen**: Discard expired food, duplicate utensils, and appliances you no longer use. Organize frequently used items for accessibility.

• **Digital Spaces**: Tidy up digital clutter by deleting unnecessary files, emails, and apps. Organize folders for quick navigation.

• **Sentimental Items**: Keep only those that evoke happy memories. Store them neatly or display a few meaningful pieces.

4. Transform the Energy of the Space

Once you've decluttered, enhance your space with tools that promote positive energy:

• **Introduce greenery**: Plants improve air quality and bring a calming natural vibe.

• **Maximize natural light**: Open curtains and clean windows to let in sunlight, which boosts mood.

• **Use scent and sound**: Aromatherapy with essential oils or soothing background music can elevate the atmosphere.

5. Maintain the Momentum

• Make decluttering a regular habit: Spend 10 minutes a day tidying up or schedule monthly decluttering sessions.

• Set boundaries for new items: Avoid impulse purchases and carefully consider whether new objects align with your goals.

Benefits of Decluttering

• **Mental clarity**: An organized space reduces cognitive load and increases focus.

• **Stress reduction**: A tidy home fosters a sense of control and calm.

• **Increased productivity**: Fewer distractions help you work more effectively.

Decluttering your physical space sets the foundation for deeper emotional and energetic cleansing, creating a harmonious environment that reflects your best self.

Simple systems for decluttering your home.

Here are simple systems for decluttering your home that are practical and easy to implement:

1. The One-Room-a-Day System

• **How it Works**: Focus on decluttering one room or area each day. Start with smaller spaces like bathrooms or entryways before tackling larger rooms like the kitchen or living room.

• **Why it Helps**: Keeps the process manageable and reduces overwhelm.

• **Tip**: Use a checklist to track your progress, celebrating each completed space.

2. The 20-Minute Rule

• **How it Works**: Dedicate just 20 minutes a day to decluttering. Set a timer, and work on one specific task, like organizing a single drawer or clearing a tabletop.

• **Why it Helps**: Makes decluttering feel less daunting and easier to fit into busy schedules.

• **Tip**: Stop when the timer ends to prevent burnout.

3. The Four-Box Method

• **How it Works**: Place four boxes labeled *Keep, Donate, Trash, Recycle* in the room you're decluttering. Sort every item into one of the boxes.

• **Why it Helps**: Forces you to make decisions about each item and ensures nothing is left behind.

• **Tip**: Commit to donating or disposing of items in the respective boxes within 24 hours to avoid second-guessing.

4. The One-In, One-Out System

• **How it Works**: For every new item you bring into your home, remove an old one.

• **Why it Helps**: Maintains balance and prevents clutter from reaccumulating.

• **Tip**: Apply this rule not only to physical items but also digital ones like apps or files.

5. The KonMari Method

• **How it Works**: Tidy by category (e.g., clothes, books, papers, sentimental items) rather than by room. Keep only items that "spark joy" and thank the rest before discarding them.

- **Why it Helps**: Encourages mindfulness and a deeper connection with your belongings.

- **Tip**: Start with less sentimental categories to build momentum.

6. The Decluttering Checklist System

- **How it Works**: Create a list of decluttering tasks broken down by room and category (e.g., "clear kitchen counters," "sort through winter coats"). Tackle one task at a time.

- **Why it Helps**: Provides a clear roadmap and reduces decision fatigue.

- **Tip**: Prioritize areas you use most often for an immediate sense of relief.

7. The "Does It Add Value?" Approach

- **How it Works**: Ask yourself, "Does this item add value to my life?" If not, let it go.

- **Why it Helps**: Simplifies decision-making and focuses on the purpose of each item.

- **Tip**: Be honest about items you've kept out of guilt or obligation.

8. The Seasonal Swap System

- **How it Works**: Declutter seasonally by reviewing clothes, décor, and other items relevant to the current time of year.

- **Why it Helps**: Reduces the effort needed to manage all belongings at once.

- **Tip**: Store out-of-season items neatly to revisit later.

By adopting one or a combination of these systems, you can declutter systematically without feeling overwhelmed. The key is consistency—regular efforts lead to a lasting, clutter-free environment.

Tips for identifying "energy blockages" like old or unused items.

Identifying "energy blockages" in your home often involves recognizing items and spaces that feel heavy, stagnant, or emotionally draining. Here are some practical tips to help pinpoint and address these blockages:

1. Notice Areas of Neglect

• Look for spots in your home that you avoid cleaning, organizing, or spending time in. Neglected spaces often harbor stagnant energy.

• **Examples**: Cluttered closets, overstuffed drawers, or unused corners of a room.

2. Pay Attention to Emotional Reactions

• Observe how you feel in each part of your home. Areas that make you uneasy, frustrated, or tired may have energy blockages.

• **Tip**: Keep a journal to note spaces that evoke strong negative feelings or discomfort.

3. Evaluate Items You Haven't Used in a While

• Identify items you haven't touched in the past year. Unused or forgotten belongings often carry stale energy and take up mental and physical space.

• **Action Step**: Ask yourself, "Do I need this? Does it serve a purpose or bring me joy?" If not, consider letting it go.

4. Look for Visual Clutter

• Too many items in one area—like crowded bookshelves, countertops, or walls—can overwhelm the senses and block the flow of positive energy.

• **Tip**: Focus on creating open, balanced spaces with minimal visual noise.

5. Inspect Broken or Damaged Items

• Broken objects or appliances can symbolize unresolved issues and stagnant energy in your life.

• **Action Step**: Repair items you value or discard those that are no longer functional.

6. Be Mindful of Sentimental Attachments

• Sentimental objects can carry emotional weight, especially if they're tied to difficult memories or relationships.

• **Tip**: Keep items that bring joy or positive memories, and consider releasing those that anchor you to the past.

7. Consider Energy Flow in Each Room

• Walk through your home and note where furniture placement feels cramped or blocks movement. Poor room layout can disrupt energy circulation (similar to Feng Shui principles).

• **Action Step**: Rearrange furniture to promote openness and accessibility.

8. Observe Clutter Hotspots

• Piles of mail, stacks of papers, or items regularly left in disorganized heaps are telltale signs of energetic congestion.

• **Action Step**: Dedicate 5-10 minutes daily to clearing these zones.

9. Check Forgotten Storage Spaces

• Basements, attics, garages, and storage units are often "dumping grounds" for unused items. These areas can hold stagnant energy if not addressed periodically.

• **Tip**: Regularly sort through storage spaces to release items that no longer serve you.

10. Trust Your Intuition

• Sometimes, you can sense when something feels "off" about an object or space, even if you can't pinpoint why. Trust these feelings—they're often tied to the energy of the area or item.

By identifying and clearing these energy blockages, you can restore balance, invite positivity, and create a harmonious home environment.

Chapter 3

Cleansing Rituals for Your Home

Cleansing rituals help remove negative or stagnant energy and invite positive, vibrant energy into your living space. These practices combine ancient traditions with modern techniques, offering both spiritual and practical benefits.

1. Smudging with Sage or Palo Santo

• **What It Does**: Smudging clears negative energy and purifies the air.

• **How to Do It**: Light a bundle of sage or a palo santo stick until it smolders, then walk through your home, wafting the smoke into corners, doorways, and windows. Set a positive intention as you go (e.g., "I release all negativity and welcome peace").

• **Pro Tip**: Open windows to allow negative energy to leave as you cleanse.

• **Origins**: Smudging is rooted in Native American and other indigenous practices. Use these tools respectfully.

2. Salt Cleansing

• **What It Does**: Salt absorbs negative energy and creates protective boundaries.

• **How to Do It**:

○ Sprinkle sea salt in the corners of each room and let it sit for 24 hours before vacuuming or sweeping.

○ Place bowls of salt near windows or doors to block incoming negativity.

○ Use a saltwater spray (dissolve salt

Techniques using sage, palo santo, and other tools.

Here are various techniques using tools like sage, palo santo, and others to energetically cleanse your home:

1. Smudging with Sage

• **Purpose**: Clears negative energy, resets the energy in a space, and promotes peace.

• **How to Use**:

1 Light the end of a sage bundle until it smolders, producing smoke.

2 Gently blow out the flame.

3 Hold the bundle over a fireproof dish to catch ashes.

4 Walk through your home in a clockwise direction, starting at the entrance. Focus on corners, doorways, and windows where stagnant energy tends to accumulate.

5 Set an intention, such as "I release all negative energy and welcome positivity."

6 Extinguish the sage in sand or a fireproof container.

2. Burning Palo Santo

• **Purpose**: Invites positivity and cleanses lighter energy rather than purging deeply negative energy.

• **How to Use**:

1 Light one end of the palo santo stick until it produces smoke.

2 Move the smoke through the room, paying special attention to areas where energy feels heavy.

3 Allow the stick to smolder and extinguish itself or gently press it into a fireproof dish to put it out.

3. Using Essential Oils

• **Purpose**: Cleanses and energizes the space while adding a pleasant scent.

• **How to Use**:

o Add oils like lavender, frankincense, or eucalyptus to a diffuser and let it run in the room.

o Mix a few drops of cleansing essential oils in a spray bottle with water and mist the space.

4. Incense Cleansing

• **Purpose**: Similar to smudging, incense is used to clear spaces and imbue a room with sacred energy.

• **How to Use**:

o Light incense sticks made from natural materials like sandalwood or cedar.

o Place them in an incense holder and allow the smoke to drift through the space.

5. Candle Rituals

• **Purpose**: Removes heavy energy while symbolizing light and clarity.

• **How to Use**:

○ Light a white candle for purity and peace.

○ Move the candle through the home (carefully), focusing on areas that feel dark or heavy.

○ Say a cleansing affirmation such as, "This light clears all negativity and fills this space with love."

6. Sound Clearing

• **Purpose**: Breaks up stagnant energy using vibrations.

• **How to Use**:

○ Ring a bell, chime, or Tibetan singing bowl in each corner of the room.

○ Clap your hands or use a drum to disrupt dense energy.

○ Follow this with silence or soothing music to stabilize the energy.

7. Crystals

• **Purpose**: Absorbs negative energy and emits positive vibrations.

• **How to Use**:

○ Place black tourmaline or obsidian at entry points to block negativity.

○ Use clear quartz or selenite in the center of the room for purification.

Best Practices

• **Open Windows**: Always open windows or doors to allow the released energy to leave your space.

• **Set Intentions**: As you cleanse, focus on positive affirmations or visualizations of a peaceful, harmonious home.

• **Respect Cultural Origins**: Understand and honor the cultural significance of tools like sage and palo santo, using them responsibly and sustainably.

These techniques are flexible and can be customized to suit your preferences or the specific needs of your space.

How to make your own cleansing sprays with essential oils.

Making your own cleansing sprays with essential oils is a simple and effective way to purify your space and bring positive energy into your home. Here's a guide on how to create your own sprays:

Basic Recipe for a Cleansing Spray

Ingredients:

• 1 cup distilled water

• 1 tablespoon witch hazel or vodka (to help the oils mix with water)

• 20-30 drops of essential oils (based on your preference)

Instructions:

1 Combine Water and Witch Hazel/Vodka: In a spray bottle, combine 1 cup of distilled water with 1 tablespoon of witch hazel or vodka. This acts as an emulsifier and helps the oils mix into the water.

2 Add Essential Oils: Choose essential oils known for their cleansing properties. A few good combinations include:

○ **Lavender and Frankincense** for relaxation and purification.

○ **Lemon, Peppermint, and Eucalyptus** for refreshing and energizing energy.

○ **Sage or Palo Santo** (or even a combination) for deep energetic cleansing.

3 Shake Well: Cap the bottle and shake it vigorously to mix the oils with the water.

4 Spray: Lightly mist the spray around your space, focusing on corners, doorways, and areas that feel heavy or stagnant.

Essential Oil Blends for Different Energetic Purposes

• **For Purification**:

○ 20 drops **Sage**

○ 15 drops **Lemon**

○ 10 drops **Lavender**

(*These oils help clear negativity and purify the energy in your home.*)

• **For Calm and Peace**:

○ 15 drops **Lavender**

○ 10 drops **Chamomile**

○ 5 drops **Rose**

(*Perfect for creating a peaceful, calming environment.*)

- **For Energizing**:

○ 10 drops **Peppermint**

○ 10 drops **Lemon**

○ 5 drops **Eucalyptus**

(*This combination lifts the energy and refreshes the space.*)

- **For Protection**:

○ 15 drops **Frankincense**

○ 10 drops **Cedarwood**

○ 5 drops **Black Spruce**

(*Ideal for creating a protective barrier against negativity.*)

Optional Add-ins

- **Crystals**: Add small crystals like **clear quartz** or **amethyst** to the bottle to enhance the energetic properties of your spray.

- **Rose Water**: Use rose water as an alternative to distilled water for added freshness and spiritual benefits.

Tips

- **Shake Before Use**: Essential oils can separate from the water, so make sure to shake the bottle before each use.

- **Test on Fabric**: Before spraying on delicate fabrics, do a patch test to avoid staining.

- **Avoid Over-spraying**: Mist lightly in each room to create a subtle cleansing effect without overwhelming the space with scent.

By making your own cleansing spray, you can create an energetically aligned environment using natural, non-toxic ingredients. Enjoy the ritual of clearing your space with scents that resonate with your intentions!

Rituals for resetting the energy after conflict or stress.

Resetting the energy in your space after conflict or stress is essential for creating a peaceful environment and restoring balance. Below are a few rituals and techniques you can use to shift the energy:

1. Smudging Ritual (Sage, Palo Santo, or Lavender)

• **How It Works**: Smudging is an ancient practice used to clear negative or stagnant energy. After a stressful event or argument, the smoke from sage, palo santo, or even lavender helps to neutralize the energy and bring in fresh, positive vibrations.

• **Steps**:

1 Light your chosen smudge stick and let it smolder, producing smoke.

2 Walk through your home, starting at the entrance and moving clockwise. Focus on corners and areas where the energy feels heavy.

3 Set a positive intention, such as "I release all negativity and invite peace and calm into this space."

4 Open windows to allow the old energy to escape.

2. Sound Clearing (Bells, Chimes, or Singing Bowls)

• **How It Works**: Sound vibrations help to break up stagnant or negative energy and restore harmony. Singing bowls, bells, or chimes are particularly effective at shifting energy and resetting the space after tension.

• **Steps**:

1 Use a Tibetan singing bowl, bell, or chime to make soothing sounds.

2 Move through the room slowly, allowing the sound to reach all corners and areas where the energy feels stuck.

3 If you don't have a singing bowl or bell, clapping your hands or using a drum can also work to break up dense energy.

4 Follow with silence or soft, calming music to stabilize the new energy.

3. Salt Cleansing

• **How It Works**: Salt is known for its purifying and protective properties. After a conflict, it can help absorb negativity and bring back a sense of balance.

• **Steps**:

1 Sprinkle sea salt in the corners of the room and leave it for a few hours or overnight.

2 Sweep or vacuum the salt the next day, imagining that you are sweeping out any residual negative energy.

3 Alternatively, you can place bowls of salt near doorways to absorb negative energy entering the space.

4. Candle Ritual for Peace

• **How It Works**: Light has a symbolic connection to peace and healing. A candle lit with the intention of calming the space can help reset the energy.

- **Steps**:

1 Light a white or pale blue candle to symbolize purity, calm, and peace.

2 As the candle burns, focus on positive affirmations like, "I invite calm and clarity into this space."

3 Allow the candle to burn for a short time as a sign of resetting the energy, and extinguish it safely when finished.

5. Visualization and Affirmations

- **How It Works**: Using visualization techniques can help reset emotional and energetic patterns in the space. Affirmations reinforce your intention for healing and peace.

- **Steps**:

1 Sit quietly, close your eyes, and take deep breaths. Visualize the space filled with a warm, golden light.

2 Imagine this light pushing out any negative energy and filling the room with peace.

3 Recite positive affirmations, such as, "This space is calm and filled with love and harmony," or "I release all tension and welcome tranquility."

4 Repeat this for 5-10 minutes.

6. Cleansing with Water

- **How It Works**: Water is known to purify and reset energy. This is why people often cleanse with water during rituals for healing or release.

- **Steps**:

1 Fill a bowl with water, adding a few drops of cleansing essential oils (e.g., lavender, eucalyptus, or lemon).

2 Use a cloth or your hands to dip into the water and wipe down surfaces, especially in areas where the energy feels heavy.

3 Imagine the water absorbing all negative energy, leaving the space clean and clear.

7. Open Windows to Let Energy Flow

• **How It Works**: Stale air can trap negative energy, so opening windows allows fresh air to circulate and reset the energetic flow in your home.

• **Steps**:

1 Open windows wide and let fresh air flow through the space.

2 As you open the windows, visualize the negative energy leaving with the breeze.

3 This simple ritual helps promote the flow of positive energy and new beginnings.

8. Feng Shui Remedies

• **How It Works**: Feng Shui is a traditional Chinese practice that emphasizes the flow of energy (Chi) through a space. After conflict or stress, certain Feng Shui remedies can be used to reset the energy.

• **Steps**:

1 Ensure that the space is free of clutter, as this blocks the flow of positive energy.

2 Use mirrors to reflect light and create balance, and introduce plants to bring vibrant energy into the room.

3 Arrange furniture in a way that promotes harmony, such as having seating that allows you to see the door without sitting directly in line with it.

By using these rituals and practices, you can help reset the energy in your home after stress or conflict, inviting healing, peace, and balance into your space. Each technique aligns with creating a sacred, balanced atmosphere that promotes emotional clarity and well-being.

Chapter 4

Cultivating Positive Energy

Cultivating positive energy in your home and life is essential for maintaining harmony, peace, and personal well-being. There are several practices and habits that can help you invite and maintain positivity in your environment and mind.

1. Create a Harmonious Environment

• **Decluttering**: Physical clutter can block the flow of energy (Chi) in your space. By regularly decluttering and organizing, you allow energy to flow freely, creating a sense of calm and order. Feng Shui principles emphasize the importance of a clutter-free environment to encourage positive energy.

• **Lighting and Airflow**: Natural light is a powerful source of positivity. Ensure your home is well-lit, especially with sunlight, and open windows to let fresh air flow, which can lift the energy in your space.

2. Mindful Use of Plants and Nature

• **Houseplants**: Plants are not only aesthetically pleasing, but they are also believed to bring good energy into a space. Indoor plants like peace lilies, jade plants, and snake plants help purify the air and symbolize growth and vitality. Feng Shui recommends placing plants in areas where energy flow is crucial, such as the center of a room or near the entrance.

• **Natural Elements**: Incorporating natural materials (wood, stone, water features) in your decor can connect you with nature and promote grounding energy.

3. Practicing Gratitude

• **Daily Affirmations**: Incorporating gratitude into your daily routine can shift your mindset and invite positivity. Saying affirmations like "I am thankful for all the abundance in my life" or "I am surrounded by love and light" helps cultivate a sense of appreciation and abundance.

• **Gratitude Journals**: Writing down things you are grateful for daily can help you focus on the positive aspects of your life, which can shift your mental energy to a more positive vibration.

4. Cleansing Rituals

• **Smudging with Sage or Palo Santo**: As mentioned earlier, smudging is a common practice to clear negative energy. The smoke from sacred herbs like sage, palo santo, and lavender is believed to neutralize harmful vibrations and promote healing and tranquility.

• **Essential Oil Diffusers**: Using essential oils like lavender, frankincense, or lemon in a diffuser can purify the air and infuse your space with positive energy. These scents are known for their calming, purifying, and uplifting properties.

5. Intention Setting and Meditation

• **Setting Positive Intentions**: Begin each day by setting a positive intention, such as "Today, I invite peace, love, and success into my life." This practice helps to focus your energy in a productive and positive direction.

• **Meditation**: Regular meditation is an excellent way to connect with your inner self and cultivate peace and positivity. Guided meditations focused on healing, grounding, and positivity can be especially effective in resetting energy.

6. Surround Yourself with Positive People

• **Social Energy**: The people you interact with deeply influence your energy. Surrounding yourself with individuals who uplift you, support your growth, and share a positive outlook can increase your own energy levels. Conversely, distancing yourself from negative or toxic people helps protect your energy.

• **Acts of Kindness**: Small acts of kindness, like offering compliments or helping others, can raise both your energy and theirs, creating a ripple effect of positivity.

7. Regular Movement and Exercise

• **Physical Activity**: Moving your body is a powerful way to release pent-up energy and boost your mood. Yoga, dance, or even regular walks can help circulate energy, release tension, and promote a sense of well-being.

• **Breathing Exercises**: Practicing deep breathing can help reset your energy, lower stress levels, and improve your mental clarity.

8. Sound Healing

• **Sound Baths**: Instruments like singing bowls, chimes, or bells can be used to clear stagnant energy and reset the vibrational frequency of a space. Sound therapy helps in balancing emotional and physical energy and can promote healing.

• **Music**: Listening to uplifting or calming music helps shift your emotional state, increasing feelings of joy and relaxation.

By incorporating these practices into your daily life, you can begin to cultivate a space and mindset filled with positive energy, which can have a lasting impact on your well-being and overall outlook. Regularly practicing these rituals and habits will create a vibrant, peaceful environment where positivity can thrive.

Incorporating plants, crystals, and water features to enhance good vibes.

Incorporating plants, crystals, and water features into your space can significantly enhance the positive energy in your environment. Each of these elements has its own unique properties that contribute to creating a harmonious and uplifting atmosphere.

1. Plants

Plants are powerful tools for improving both the physical and energetic environment of your home. They help purify the air, reduce stress, and create a sense of tranquility. According to Feng Shui, plants are especially beneficial in the home, as they symbolize growth, vitality, and health. The presence of plants can balance the energy and promote feelings of calm.

Best Plants for Positive Energy:

• **Peace Lily**: Known for purifying the air, the peace lily also brings calm energy and is often used in Feng Shui to clear negative energy and promote relaxation.

• **Snake Plant**: This resilient plant is believed to absorb toxins and improve air quality, while also promoting a peaceful atmosphere.

• **Jade Plant**: Considered a symbol of prosperity and good luck, the jade plant can help attract positive energy into the home.

• **Aloe Vera**: Besides its healing properties for the skin, aloe vera is known for its energy-clearing abilities and is said to bring good fortune.

Plant Placement Tips:

• Place plants in the **east or southeast** corners of your home to foster good health and wealth (according to Feng Shui).

• Keep plants in the **living room or near the entrance** to welcome good energy and offer protection.

2. Crystals

Crystals have long been used for their energetic properties to cleanse, heal, and balance the energy of a space. Certain crystals can amplify good vibes and help dispel negative energy.

Popular Crystals for Positive Energy:

• **Clear Quartz**: Known as a powerful cleanser and amplifier of positive energy, clear quartz can be placed throughout the home to enhance the vibrational frequency.

• **Amethyst**: This calming stone is said to promote emotional balance and spiritual growth. It's commonly placed in areas where you want to cultivate peace and tranquility.

• **Rose Quartz**: Known as the stone of love, rose quartz fosters compassion, love, and harmony. It can help to soften the energy in a room and promote positive relationships.

• **Citrine**: This golden-yellow stone is considered to bring abundance and positivity, attracting good fortune and success. It's perfect for the prosperity corner (southeast) of your home.

Crystal Placement Tips:

• **Clear Quartz** can be placed in the **center of a room** to help clear and amplify energy.

• **Amethyst** works well in the **bedroom** or **meditation space** to promote calm and relaxation.

• **Rose Quartz** is best placed near relationships or **living areas** to enhance love and harmony.

• **Citrine** should be placed in the **prosperity corner** of the home (southeast corner).

3. Water Features

Water is a symbol of abundance, flow, and prosperity. It is believed to attract positive energy and enhance the flow of Chi (life force) in your environment. The sound of moving water can also have a soothing effect, helping to reduce stress and promote a sense of peace and relaxation.

Types of Water Features:

• **Fountains**: A small indoor fountain or water bowl can help circulate energy in your home while providing a calming sound that promotes tranquility.

• **Aquariums**: In Feng Shui, aquariums are thought to attract prosperity, especially if they feature goldfish or flowing water.

• **Waterfalls**: Small tabletop waterfalls or wall-mounted water features offer the benefits of sound therapy and energy circulation.

Water Feature Placement Tips:

• Place fountains in the **living room** or **near entrances** to invite wealth and positive energy into the home.

• Water features can also be placed in the **east** or **southeast** areas of your home to promote good health and abundance.

• Avoid placing water features in the **bedroom** or **kitchen**, as these are considered spaces for rest or nourishment, not flow and movement.

Benefits of Combining Plants, Crystals, and Water Features

When combined, plants, crystals, and water features create a balanced and harmonious environment. The plants purify the air and bring life, the crystals add healing energy, and the water features promote prosperity and calmness. By integrating all three, you can create an energy-rich space that supports physical, emotional, and spiritual well-being.

• **A peaceful and calming energy** is fostered through the combination of soothing plants like peace lilies with calming amethyst or rose quartz crystals.

• **Abundance and prosperity** are encouraged by adding citrine crystals, jade plants, and small water features.

• **Emotional healing** can be supported with rose quartz and soothing plants like aloe vera, complemented by the sound of a gentle fountain.

By incorporating these elements thoughtfully, you can create a sanctuary that enhances your well-being and nurtures a positive, uplifting atmosphere.

The role of light, color, and aroma in creating harmony.

The role of **light, color, and aroma** in creating harmony within a space is deeply tied to both emotional and psychological well-being. These elements can profoundly influence how we feel, think, and behave in our surroundings. By carefully considering and incorporating them into your home or workplace, you can create a balanced and harmonious atmosphere that supports your mental, physical, and emotional health.

1. Light

Light is essential in shaping the energy of a space. It has the power to lift moods, increase productivity, and even influence our physical health. There are two primary types of light to consider: **natural light** and **artificial light**.

• **Natural Light**: Exposure to natural sunlight boosts serotonin levels, which can improve mood and help with sleep regulation. Sunlight also connects us to natural cycles, creating a grounding and calming effect. When possible, open windows and allow natural light to flood the room. Additionally, natural light is often linked to better indoor air quality, as it promotes airflow.

• **Artificial Light**: The type of artificial lighting you choose can also have a significant impact. **Warm lights** (yellow tones) tend to create a cozy, relaxing atmosphere, ideal for living rooms or bedrooms, while **cool lights** (blue or white tones) are better for focused work and productivity in spaces like offices or kitchens. Adjustable lighting, such as dimmable bulbs, can offer flexibility and ensure the room's lighting is always conducive to the mood you wish to set.

Sources:

• "Lighting and Mood: How to Use It to Your Advantage," Psychology Today

• "The Power of Natural Light," Harvard Health Publishing

2. Color

Colors in a room do more than just enhance its aesthetic appeal—they can affect our emotions, energy levels, and even behavior. **Color psychology** is a field that explores how different colors influence our thoughts and feelings.

• **Warm Colors**: Colors like **red, orange, and yellow** can stimulate energy and creativity, but they can also induce feelings of warmth, excitement, and passion. These colors are often used in dining rooms or home offices where energy and activity are desired. However, in large doses, they can also feel overwhelming, so moderation is key.

• **Cool Colors**: **Blue, green, and purple** are considered calming and peaceful. Blue is associated with tranquility, focus, and clarity, making it ideal for bedrooms and study areas. Green, representing nature and growth, can be used in living spaces to create balance and refresh the atmosphere. Purple evokes spirituality and creativity, so it works well in meditation or artistic spaces.

• **Neutral Colors**: Colors like **white, gray, beige, and brown** create a serene, grounded atmosphere. They are ideal for creating a backdrop that allows other elements (like plants, artwork, or furniture) to stand out. These tones are often used in minimalistic designs or to bring a sense of sophistication and calm.

Sources:

• "Color Psychology: The Effects of Colors on the Mind," Verywell Mind

• "How Color Affects Your Mood and Emotions," The Spruce

3. Aroma

Aromas, like color, influence our moods and emotions. Scent can trigger memories, comfort, and relaxation or even inspire creativity and focus. Using **essential oils**, candles, or incense can fill a space with positive, calming energy.

• **Lavender**: Known for its calming properties, lavender is often used to promote relaxation, reduce anxiety, and help with sleep. It's ideal for bedrooms or spaces where you unwind, like reading nooks.

• **Citrus Scents**: Essential oils like **lemon**, **orange**, and **grapefruit** are refreshing and energizing. They are excellent for creating an uplifting atmosphere in kitchens, living rooms, or workspaces.

• **Sandalwood and Frankincense**: These deeper, earthy scents are known for grounding and calming effects. They help clear negative energy and bring clarity, which is why they are often used in meditation spaces or areas where focus is needed.

• **Peppermint**: A stimulating scent, peppermint can improve concentration and alertness. It's perfect for offices or study areas.

Sources:

• "The Science of Scent: How Smell Affects Our Mood," Psychology Today

• "How Essential Oils Affect the Body and Mind," Mayo Clinic

Combining Light, Color, and Aroma for Harmony

When combined, light, color, and aroma can create a powerful, multi-sensory experience that promotes harmony and balance. Here are some ways to integrate these elements together:

• **Relaxation Space**: Use soft **warm light** (e.g., yellow-toned lamps), soothing **blue or green colors** for the walls, and calming **lavender or sandalwood scents** to create a peaceful retreat in your bedroom or meditation room.

• **Productivity Zone**: Bright, cool **white or blue lighting** combined with energizing **orange or yellow accents** and **citrus aromas** can stimulate focus and motivation in your home office or study area.

• **Social Spaces**: Use **neutral tones** with some **red or purple** accents for warmth, paired with a **peppermint** or **frankincense** diffuser to foster conversation and creativity in your living or dining room.

By thoughtfully using light, color, and aroma in your home or workspace, you can tailor the environment to promote relaxation, productivity, or creativity, creating harmony and improving overall well-being.

Chapter 5

Personal Energy Detox

A **personal energy detox** is the process of cleansing your physical, emotional, and mental state to remove negative energy, recharge, and restore balance. In today's fast-paced, often stressful world, it's easy to accumulate emotional and mental "toxins" that can drain your vitality. Detoxing your personal energy can help you feel more centered, focused, and empowered.

Here are several ways to effectively detox your energy:

1. Physical Detox: Cleanse Your Body

Physical health directly influences your energy levels. To detox your body and restore vitality, consider:

• **Hydration**: Drinking plenty of water helps flush toxins from your body and keeps energy flowing freely. Infusing water with lemon or mint can add extra detoxifying properties.

• **Nourishing Foods**: Eating whole, nutrient-dense foods like fruits, vegetables, and lean proteins can support your body's natural detoxification processes. Avoid processed foods, sugar, and alcohol, which can deplete energy.

• **Exercise**: Movement, especially yoga, walking, or dance, can help release trapped energy, stimulate blood flow, and clear mental fog. Regular exercise also enhances mood and energy levels by releasing endorphins.

• **Sleep**: Quality sleep is essential for recharging your body and mind. Aim for 7-9 hours of restful sleep per night to allow your energy to regenerate.

2. Emotional Detox: Release Negative Emotions

Negative emotions like anger, sadness, fear, and resentment can create energetic blockages. To detox emotionally:

• **Journaling**: Writing down your thoughts and emotions can help you process and release them. By articulating your feelings, you bring them out of your body and mind, allowing space for new, positive energy.

• **Forgiveness**: Holding on to grudges and unresolved anger drains your energy. Practicing forgiveness, even if it's just for your own peace of mind, can lighten your emotional load.

• **Meditation**: Meditation and mindfulness practices allow you to become aware of your thoughts and emotions, giving you the tools to release negativity and shift your mindset to a more positive state.

• **Therapy or Energy Healing**: Working with a therapist or energy healer (e.g., Reiki or Emotional Freedom Technique) can help you work through emotional blockages and reset your emotional energy.

3. Mental Detox: Clear Your Mind

Mental clutter often results from overthinking, stress, and constant information overload. To detox your mind:

• **Mindfulness Practices**: Being present in the moment can help reduce mental chatter and anxiety. Practices like deep breathing, mindfulness meditation, or body scans help you stay grounded and clear.

• **Digital Detox**: Spending too much time on screens—whether on social media, email, or news sites—can overwhelm the mind. Taking breaks from technology, especially before bed, allows your mind to relax and reset.

• **Decluttering Your Space**: A cluttered physical environment can contribute to mental chaos. Cleaning and organizing your home can help you feel more focused and clear-headed.

• **Visualization**: Visualizing your ideal, calm state or imagining yourself in a peaceful, energizing environment can help you mentally detox and reset.

4. Spiritual Detox: Reconnect with Your Higher Self

Spiritual practices are integral to detoxing your energy, helping you reconnect with your higher self and restore alignment.

• **Energy Cleansing Rituals**: Smudging with sage, palo santo, or frankincense, as well as using crystals, can help cleanse negative energies from your aura and home. This can create a sense of spiritual renewal and protection.

• **Intention Setting**: Setting intentions for the day or week ahead helps guide your actions and mindset. By aligning your energy with clear, purposeful goals, you ensure that your energy remains focused and directed toward positive outcomes.

• **Spiritual Practice**: Engaging in your preferred spiritual practice, whether it's prayer, meditation, or connecting with nature, can help reset your energy and restore balance.

5. Detox Your Environment: Create a Supportive Space

The environment around you has a profound effect on your personal energy. An environment filled with clutter, harsh lighting, or negative energy can drain your vitality.

• **Create a Sacred Space**: Designating a specific area in your home for relaxation, meditation, or prayer can serve as an energetic recharge station.

• **Surround Yourself with Positive Energy**: Incorporate elements such as plants, crystals, and soft lighting to create a harmonious atmosphere. These elements can help promote peace, abundance, and clarity.

• **Sound Healing**: Playing calming music, using sound bowls, or listening to nature sounds can help restore positive vibrations to your space.

6. Practice Gratitude and Positive Thinking

Focusing on gratitude shifts your energy from lack to abundance. Regularly reflecting on the things you're grateful for can uplift your energy and bring more positivity into your life.

• **Gratitude Journal**: Write down three things you're grateful for each day. This simple practice helps shift your mindset toward positivity and encourages the flow of good energy.

• **Positive Affirmations**: Repeating affirmations such as "I am worthy of love and peace" or "I am aligned with positive energy" helps reinforce a healthy and balanced mindset.

. . .

By incorporating these practices into your daily routine, you can significantly improve your energy, remove stagnation, and invite more positivity into your life. The goal of a personal energy detox is to create space for renewal, balance, and growth, so you can feel more centered, vibrant, and empowered in your everyday life.

Practices like meditation, breathwork, and journaling to release negativity.

Practices like **meditation**, **breathwork**, and **journaling** are highly effective tools for releasing negativity and promoting emotional well-being. These practices allow you to address accumulated stress, negative emotions, and mental clutter. Here's how each practice works and how it can help detoxify your personal energy:

1. Meditation: Clearing the Mind and Restoring Balance

Meditation is one of the most powerful ways to release negativity. It encourages stillness, presence, and deep self-awareness, helping you to process emotions and reset your mental state.

• **Mindfulness Meditation**: This practice involves focusing on the present moment without judgment. By observing your thoughts and emotions without getting caught up in them, you create a sense of detachment and clarity. This helps to neutralize negative thought patterns and promotes emotional balance.

• **Guided Meditation**: In guided meditations, practitioners follow the voice of a guide, which often involves visualizing healing energy, white light, or other images meant to cleanse the mind and spirit. Many guided meditations focus on releasing stress, clearing emotional blockages, and inviting positive energy.

• **Loving-Kindness Meditation (Metta)**: This type of meditation focuses on cultivating feelings of love and compassion toward oneself and others. By releasing anger, resentment, and fear through compassion, it can help dissolve negativity and open up your heart.

Benefits: Meditation has been shown to reduce stress, enhance emotional regulation, and lower levels of anxiety and depression (Harvard Health, Mayo Clinic).

2. Breathwork: Releasing Tension Through Conscious Breathing

Breathwork involves controlled breathing exercises that promote relaxation and help release stored tension in the body. By focusing on the breath, you activate the parasympathetic nervous system (responsible for rest and relaxation), which helps to reduce stress and clear emotional blockages.

• **Box Breathing**: This technique involves inhaling, holding the breath, exhaling, and holding again, each for a count of four. Box breathing calms the nervous system and promotes emotional stability.

• **Alternate Nostril Breathing (Nadi Shodhana)**: This ancient practice involves breathing through one nostril at a time, alternating between nostrils while breathing deeply. It is believed to balance the energy channels in the body, harmonizing the mind and emotions.

• **Deep Belly Breathing**: This practice involves taking slow, deep breaths into the diaphragm, expanding the belly. It helps to release stress and tension from the body and calms the mind.

Benefits: Breathwork can reduce cortisol levels (the stress hormone), improve focus, and help release deep-seated emotional tension (Psychology Today, Healthline).

3. Journaling: Processing and Releasing Emotions

Journaling is an effective method for releasing negativity, as it provides an outlet for expressing and processing thoughts and emotions. Writing things down can help you gain perspective, understand your feelings, and release pent-up energy.

• **Free Writing**: Simply writing without judgment or concern for grammar can help you pour out your thoughts. By putting your feelings on paper, you release negative emotions and gain clarity on what might be weighing you down.

• **Gratitude Journaling**: Focusing on what you're grateful for shifts your energy from negative to positive. Writing down three things you're grateful for each day helps to change your mindset and cultivate a sense of abundance and joy.

• **Emotional Release Writing**: Sometimes known as "expressive writing," this practice involves writing about difficult or painful emotions. Research has shown that writing about traumatic experiences can help reduce their emotional charge and lead to healing.

Benefits: Journaling can lower stress, enhance emotional intelligence, and improve mental health by providing a safe space to explore feelings (American Psychological Association, National Institute of Health).

Incorporating These Practices Together

• **Morning Ritual**: Start your day with a short meditation to clear your mind, followed by some breathwork to energize your body. End the session with gratitude journaling to focus on the positive aspects of your life.

- **Evening Routine**: Before bed, practice deep breathing to release the stress of the day, followed by a reflective journaling session to process emotions. End with a short meditation to calm your mind and prepare for restful sleep.

By incorporating meditation, breathwork, and journaling into your daily routine, you create a holistic approach to releasing negativity and restoring balance to your energy. These practices foster emotional clarity, mental peace, and physical relaxation, empowering you to lead a more harmonious and positive life.

Creating boundaries to protect your energy.

Creating boundaries to protect your energy is essential for maintaining emotional, mental, and physical well-being. Boundaries help you preserve your personal space, safeguard against negative influences, and maintain balance in relationships. Here are some practical steps to establish healthy boundaries and protect your energy:

1. Understand Your Needs and Limits

Before setting boundaries, it's important to understand your emotional and physical limits. This involves reflecting on what drains your energy and what nourishes it. Some common signs of energy depletion include feeling exhausted, irritable, or overwhelmed after social interactions or certain activities. Identifying these patterns will help you create boundaries that support your well-being.

- **Self-awareness**: Recognize what situations, people, or environments leave you feeling drained.

- **Self-care**: Prioritize activities that recharge you, such as rest, nature walks, meditation, or creative pursuits.

Sources:

• "The Importance of Setting Boundaries for Your Mental Health," Psychology Today

• "How to Set Boundaries: A Guide to Protecting Your Energy," Mind Body Green

2. Learn to Say No

One of the most important boundary-setting skills is learning to say no. Saying no doesn't make you selfish; it's a way to protect your energy and ensure that you're not overcommitting. When you say yes to things that don't align with your values or drain your energy, you're neglecting your own needs.

• **Practice assertiveness**: Politely but firmly decline requests that don't serve your well-being. For example, "I appreciate the invitation, but I need to take care of myself today."

• **Prioritize your energy**: Focus on activities that align with your values and bring you joy.

Sources:

• "The Power of Saying No," Harvard Business Review

• "Learning to Say No and Protect Your Energy," Verywell Mind

3. Set Clear Emotional Boundaries

Emotional boundaries involve protecting yourself from taking on others' emotions or allowing yourself to become too enmeshed in their problems. This is particularly important in close relationships, where empathy can blur the lines of personal responsibility.

• **Empathy without enmeshment**: You can be empathetic and compassionate without absorbing others' emotional states.

• **Limit emotional venting**: If someone consistently vents their frustrations to you, set boundaries by telling them how it affects you and offering solutions to address it without taking on their emotions.

Sources:

• "Emotional Boundaries: How to Set Them and Why They Matter," PsychCentral

• "How to Set Healthy Emotional Boundaries in Relationships," Psychology Today

4. Create Physical Boundaries

Physical boundaries are essential for maintaining personal space. This might mean needing quiet time, creating a physical space where you can retreat, or setting limits on physical contact.

• **Personal space**: Respecting your own need for space—whether through creating a designated quiet area or simply requesting physical space in crowded settings—is a key way to preserve energy.

• **Body language**: Use body language to signal boundaries, such as stepping back from someone when you need space or using neutral responses when you're not ready to engage.

Sources:

• "How to Create Physical Boundaries for Your Health," Mind Body Green

• "Personal Boundaries: 5 Tips to Protect Your Energy," Healthline

5. Practice Energy Protection Techniques

When you feel vulnerable or drained, you can use physical or spiritual practices to protect your energy. This may involve visualization, using crystals, or performing grounding exercises.

• **Visualization**: Imagine a protective bubble of light around you that shields you from negativity. Visualize this bubble expanding to fill the space you occupy, creating a safe zone.

• **Grounding**: Stand or sit with your feet firmly on the ground and visualize yourself rooted like a tree. This helps you stay centered and less affected by external energies.

• **Crystals**: Protective stones like **black tourmaline**, **amethyst**, and **clear quartz** are believed to absorb negative energy and shield your aura.

Sources:

• "Energy Protection Techniques: How to Shield Yourself from Negative Energy," MindBodyGreen

• "How to Protect Your Energy with Crystals," The Crystal Council

6. Create Boundaries in Digital Spaces

In today's world, digital overload is a common way to drain energy. Setting boundaries in digital spaces—such as social media, emails, and texts—is crucial for protecting your energy.

• **Digital detox**: Limit the amount of time spent on social media or devices, especially in the evenings. Set time limits on your phone or use apps that help monitor screen time.

• **Unfollow or mute**: Unfollow accounts that bring negative energy or stress into your life. You can mute notifications to reduce the pressure of constant communication.

• **Set work boundaries**: Define work hours and stick to them. Avoid checking work emails or messages outside of your designated hours.

Sources:

• "How to Set Digital Boundaries and Protect Your Energy," The New York Times

• "Why Setting Digital Boundaries is Important for Mental Health," Forbes

By setting boundaries in these areas, you can protect your personal energy and maintain balance in your life. The key is to recognize when your energy is being drained and take proactive steps to recharge and preserve your well-being. Boundaries help create a sense of empowerment and ensure that you're living authentically and healthily.

Chapter 6

Daily Practices to Maintain High Vibrations

Maintaining high vibrations is about consistently engaging in practices that nurture your physical, emotional, mental, and spiritual well-being. High vibrations correlate with positive, life-affirming energy that helps you feel connected, peaceful, and full of vitality. Incorporating daily habits into your routine can help you sustain a higher frequency of energy. Here are some daily practices that can support high vibrations:

1. Start the Day with Gratitude

Gratitude is one of the quickest ways to elevate your energy. By focusing on the positives in your life, you shift your attention away from lack and invite more abundance and joy.

• **Practice**: Upon waking, list at least three things you're grateful for—whether big or small. This simple act sets a positive tone for the day and encourages an attitude of abundance.

• **Benefit**: Gratitude helps rewire the brain to focus on positivity, which increases your energy and optimism throughout the day. (Source: *Harvard Health*)

2. Hydrate with Alkaline Water or Herbal Teas

Water is essential for maintaining high energy. Hydration helps the body flush out toxins, keeps the organs functioning, and ensures the energy flow is balanced.

• **Practice**: Start your day with a glass of water, preferably alkaline, to balance your pH and boost energy levels. You can also drink herbal teas like ginger or peppermint, which are known for their cleansing properties.

• **Benefit**: Proper hydration prevents fatigue, supports digestion, and helps maintain mental clarity. (Source: *National Institutes of Health*)

3. Move Your Body

Physical activity is a powerful way to increase your vibrational frequency. Exercise releases endorphins, which elevate mood, reduce stress, and increase vitality.

• **Practice**: Engage in daily movement that feels good to you. This could be yoga, walking, dancing, or even stretching. Aim for at least 20-30 minutes of physical activity.

• **Benefit**: Regular exercise enhances circulation, boosts energy, and helps release emotional blockages. (Source: *Mayo Clinic*)

4. Meditation and Breathwork

Meditation and breathwork allow you to clear mental clutter and maintain a peaceful, centered state, which raises your vibrational frequency.

• **Practice**: Begin with a simple meditation practice, focusing on your breath or using a guided meditation for calming or energy boosting. Breathwork techniques, such as box breathing or alternate nostril breathing, are also excellent for resetting your energy.

• **Benefit**: Meditation and breathwork promote mental clarity, reduce stress, and foster inner peace, which helps you vibrate at a higher frequency. (Source: *Psychology Today*)

5. Practice Positive Affirmations

Affirmations are a way to direct your thoughts toward positive outcomes and self-belief. Repeating uplifting statements changes your mental and emotional state, raising your vibration.

• **Practice**: Choose an affirmation that resonates with you, such as "I am worthy of love and abundance," or "I attract positive energy and opportunities." Repeat it throughout the day, especially when you need a boost.

• **Benefit**: Affirmations reprogram the subconscious mind, promote self-love, and encourage optimism. (Source: *Psychology Today*)

6. Stay Connected to Nature

Spending time outdoors connects you to the Earth's natural energy, which can help ground and elevate your own energy.

• **Practice**: Go for a walk in nature, sit under a tree, or take a few moments each day to step outside and breathe fresh air. You can also practice earthing, which involves walking barefoot on grass or soil to reconnect with the Earth's electromagnetic field.

• **Benefit**: Time in nature reduces stress, enhances mood, and restores balance. Natural elements like sunlight and fresh air can help lift your vibration. (Source: *National Geographic*)

7. Eat High-Vibrational Foods

The food you eat directly influences your energy. Eating whole, plant-based foods that are rich in nutrients and antioxidants can elevate your vibrational frequency.

• **Practice**: Include fruits, vegetables, nuts, seeds, and whole grains in your meals. Limit processed foods and focus on fresh, organic produce when possible.

• **Benefit**: High-vibrational foods nourish the body, clear mental fog, and promote a sense of well-being. (Source: *The Journal of Nutritional Biochemistry*)

8. Be Mindful of Your Environment

The energy in your home or work environment can have a significant impact on your own vibrations. Creating a peaceful, clean, and nurturing space helps maintain a high vibrational frequency.

• **Practice**: Declutter your space, add plants, crystals, or soothing lighting (like candles or Himalayan salt lamps), and ensure the area is free from negative or stagnant energy.

• **Benefit**: A clean, harmonious space enhances emotional balance and supports positive energy flow. (Source: *Psychology Today*)

9. Practice Acts of Kindness

Acts of kindness, both big and small, raise your vibration and the vibration of those around you. Giving without expecting anything in return boosts feelings of connectedness and compassion.

• **Practice**: Make it a daily habit to perform small acts of kindness—whether it's offering a compliment, helping someone, or sending a thoughtful message to a loved one.

• **Benefit**: Acts of kindness foster positive energy and create a ripple effect of goodwill. (Source: *Greater Good Science Center*)

10. End the Day with Reflection

Before bed, take a few moments to reflect on your day, acknowledge your achievements, and let go of any negativity.

• **Practice**: Journaling, reflecting, or meditating before sleep helps release any pent-up stress or emotions from the day. You can also express gratitude again as you close the day.

• **Benefit**: Ending the day on a positive note ensures you rest with a peaceful mind, setting the tone for the next day. (Source: *The

Gratitude journaling.

Gratitude journaling is a powerful practice that helps shift your mindset, increase happiness, and improve overall well-being. By regularly reflecting on the things you're thankful for, you train your mind to focus on the positive aspects of life, even during challenging times. Below are some key aspects and benefits of gratitude journaling, along with helpful tips for making the most out of this practice:

The Benefits of Gratitude Journaling

1 Improves Mental Health: Gratitude journaling has been shown to reduce symptoms of depression, anxiety, and stress by encouraging a more positive outlook. Regularly focusing on positive aspects of life can counteract the tendency to ruminate on negative thoughts (Journal of Research in Personality, 2011). Practicing gratitude shifts your emotional state and can create a buffer against daily stressors.

2 Boosts Happiness and Resilience: Studies have found that expressing gratitude can enhance overall life satisfaction and increase positive emotions. It helps to build emotional resilience, making it easier to navigate life's challenges. Grateful individuals often experience increased feelings of well-being and greater optimism about the future (American Psychologist, 2003).

3 Strengthens Relationships: Gratitude journaling isn't just beneficial for your own mental health; it can also enhance your relationships. Writing down what you're grateful for about your partner, friends, or family members strengthens the bond between you. It fosters a deeper sense of appreciation, promoting a more supportive and positive atmosphere in relationships (Psychology Today).

4 Improves Sleep: People who engage in gratitude journaling before bed often report better sleep quality. The act of reflecting on positive experiences and expressing thankfulness before sleep reduces worry and promotes a calm, peaceful state of mind (Applied Psychology: Health and Well-Being, 2009).

How to Start Gratitude Journaling

1 Keep It Simple: Start by writing down three things you're grateful for each day. These can be big or small—anything that brings you joy, comfort, or peace. Over time, you may find that you naturally begin to notice more things to be thankful for throughout your day.

2 Be Specific: Rather than just saying "I'm grateful for my family," try to be specific about why you're grateful. For example, "I'm grateful for my sister's kind support when I was feeling down" or "I'm thankful for the warm, sunny weather today." The more detailed you get, the more deeply you'll experience gratitude.

3 Focus on the Positive: Even on tough days, gratitude journaling can help you find silver linings. Try to look for lessons or small victories in the challenges you face. For instance, "I'm grateful that I was able to handle stress at work today" or "I'm thankful for the strength I found during a difficult conversation."

4 Make It a Daily Habit: The key to reaping the benefits of gratitude journaling is consistency. Try to incorporate it into your daily routine—perhaps in the morning, to set the tone for your day, or at night, to reflect on the day's positive moments.

5 Use Prompts: If you're stuck on what to write about, use prompts like:

○ What made you smile today?

○ Who in your life are you grateful for, and why?

○ What is something small that made your day better?

Tips for Maintaining a Gratitude Journal

• **Keep It Positive**: Don't let your journal become a place for venting. Make it a habit to focus on gratitude, even when it feels hard.

• **Review Your Journal**: Every week or month, go back and read through your entries. This will remind you of how much you have to be grateful for and help you stay motivated.

• **Express Gratitude to Others**: Besides journaling, consider telling people directly how grateful you are for them, whether it's through a text, a note, or a conversation.

By committing to gratitude journaling, you nurture a habit of positivity that can influence all areas of your life, fostering greater emotional balance and attracting more abundance.

Additional Resources:

• *The Psychology of Gratitude* by Robert A. Emmons, which delves deeper into the science behind gratitude and its effects on well-being.

• "Gratitude: The Ultimate Stress Buster" – Psychology Today (https://www.psychologytoday.com/articles/gratitude)

Simple habits like mindful cleaning and organizing.

Incorporating simple habits like **mindful cleaning** and **organizing** can profoundly enhance your well-being by creating an environment that nurtures mental clarity, emotional balance, and positive energy. These habits help transform your home into a space that reflects your intentions and supports your overall health. Here are some ways to integrate mindful cleaning and organizing into your daily routine:

1. Clean with Intention

Mindful cleaning is about approaching the act of cleaning as a meditative and intentional practice, rather than just a task to check off. It involves being present and aware of the process, which can elevate your energy and make the task more enjoyable.

• **Practice**: As you clean, focus on the sensations—whether it's the sound of the cloth wiping surfaces, the scent of the cleaner, or the smoothness of the dusting. This mindfulness can help release built-up stress.

• **Benefit**: Mindful cleaning has been shown to reduce stress and promote a calm, centered state (Psychology Today, 2020). The process itself becomes a form of meditation, which can improve mood and foster a sense of accomplishment.

2. Organize with Purpose

Decluttering your space intentionally allows you to release stagnant energy and create room for new opportunities. When organizing, approach each item with purpose: ask yourself if it brings value, joy, or usefulness to your life.

• **Practice**: When organizing, take time to evaluate each item and ask if it aligns with your current goals, values, or needs. Only keep things that serve a purpose or bring you joy.

• **Benefit**: Regularly tidying up in this mindful way can lead to improved mental clarity and emotional calmness, as studies show a clutter-free environment promotes better focus and productivity (Harvard Business Review, 2018). It also encourages a deeper connection to your space.

3. Create a Cleaning Routine

Consistency is key for maintaining a harmonious home. Rather than waiting until your home becomes too cluttered or dirty, establish a cleaning routine that involves small, daily habits. This reduces the overwhelming feeling that often accompanies larger cleaning sessions.

• **Practice**: Break down tasks into manageable portions and assign them to different days. For instance, vacuum on Mondays, clean the kitchen on Tuesdays, and wipe down surfaces on Wednesdays. Consistency helps prevent clutter from building up and keeps the energy in your home fresh.

• **Benefit**: A consistent cleaning routine helps create a sense of control and order, which can reduce stress and promote feelings of accomplishment (American Psychological Association, 2020).

4. Infuse Positive Energy with Aromatherapy

When cleaning or organizing, you can amplify the effects of mindful cleaning by using aromatherapy to refresh your space.

Essential oils such as lavender, eucalyptus, or citrus are known to have calming or energizing effects.

• **Practice**: Use a diffuser or spray a natural essential oil blend as you clean. Lavender promotes relaxation, while citrus scents like lemon or orange uplift energy.

• **Benefit**: Aromatherapy has been linked to reduced anxiety and improved mood (The Journal of Alternative and Complementary Medicine, 2013). Adding this sensory element while you clean enhances the overall experience, making it more enjoyable and beneficial.

5. Be Grateful for Your Space

As you clean or organize, take a moment to express gratitude for the space you have. Acknowledge the comfort, protection, and opportunities your home provides. This act of gratitude can elevate your energetic connection to the environment.

• **Practice**: While cleaning, pause and silently express thanks for your space. You can also focus on each area you clean, imagining it as a space of peace and abundance.

• **Benefit**: Gratitude helps shift your energy from scarcity to abundance and invites positive energy into your environment (Greater Good Science Center, 2020). This practice can create a sense of harmony within your home.

6. Let Go of Emotional Clutter

Emotional clutter often accumulates with physical clutter. By addressing the emotional attachments you have to items while cleaning or organizing, you allow yourself to release past negative energy and make room for new, positive experiences.

- **Practice**: While decluttering, let go of items that no longer serve you emotionally. These might be old gifts, outdated clothes, or items associated with negative memories. Acknowledge any emotional ties and consciously release them.

- **Benefit**: Letting go of emotional clutter has a significant impact on mental health. Research shows that decluttering is associated with reduced feelings of anxiety and improved emotional well-being .

Chapter 7

Sacred Spaces for Healing and Manifestation

Creating sacred spaces for healing and manifestation is about intentionally designing an environment that supports your emotional, spiritual, and mental well-being. These spaces, whether within your home, outdoors, or in your mind, are places of tranquility, focus, and positive energy where you can align with your intentions, release negative emotions, and invite healing. Here's how to create and maintain such spaces:

1. Choose the Right Location

A sacred space should feel private, safe, and comfortable. Whether you choose a corner of a room, a garden nook, or a spot in nature, it's essential that this space makes you feel calm and focused. Avoid areas of high traffic or places that are cluttered or noisy.

• **Tip**: If you're creating a sacred space indoors, look for a quiet corner or a place near natural light. If you're outdoors, find a secluded spot where you can feel at peace with nature.

• **Benefit**: A designated area helps you connect with your inner self and provides a sense of calm, making it easier to practice healing or manifestation (American Psychological Association, 2020).

2. Cleanse the Energy

Before setting up your sacred space, cleanse the energy to remove any stagnant or negative vibrations. This can be done using various methods such as smudging, sound healing, or visualizing the space being bathed in light.

• **Methods**:

○ **Smudging**: Use sage, palo santo, or sweetgrass to purify the space. The smoke is believed to clear out negative energy.

○ **Sound Healing**: Use singing bowls, chimes, or even bells to reset the energy.

○ **Visualizing**: Imagine a bright, healing light filling the room, removing all negative energy.

• **Benefit**: Cleansing your space ensures that the environment is energetically aligned with your healing or manifestation goals (Psychology Today, 2019).

3. Set Your Intentions

A sacred space becomes a powerful tool for manifestation when you infuse it with clear intentions. What do you want to manifest or heal? Write down your intentions or speak them out loud. You can also use symbols, crystals, or objects that resonate with your desires.

• **Tip**: Use affirmations or mantras that support your intentions. Place these written intentions on an altar or table in your sacred space.

- **Benefit**: Having a focused intention provides direction and helps channel your energy towards the goals you wish to manifest (Harvard Health, 2018).

4. Add Meaningful Items

Fill your sacred space with objects that help you feel spiritually nourished. These can include crystals, candles, flowers, incense, or sacred texts. Each item should serve a symbolic purpose and support your intention for healing or manifestation.

- **Crystals**: Rose quartz for love, amethyst for spiritual growth, citrine for abundance, or black tourmaline for protection.

- **Candles**: Light candles to represent illumination, transformation, or to create an atmosphere of calm.

- **Benefit**: Objects that resonate with your goals act as visual reminders of your intentions and help to reinforce positive energy in the space (MindBodyGreen, 2020).

5. Incorporate Nature

Nature is a powerful force for healing. Bringing elements of nature into your sacred space can enhance your connection to the earth and help manifest your desires.

- **Methods**:

o **Plants**: Choose plants known for their healing properties, such as aloe vera or peace lilies. They purify the air and add life to your space.

o **Water Features**: A small fountain or bowl of water can symbolize flow and abundance.

o **Natural Light**: Sunlight brings vitality and growth. If possible, position your sacred space near a window or outdoor setting.

• **Benefit**: Nature promotes grounding, balance, and a connection to the Earth's energy, all of which support healing and manifestation (National Geographic, 2020).

6. Practice Regular Rituals

To maintain the healing energy of your sacred space, establish regular practices that keep the space alive with positive energy. This could include daily meditation, journaling, prayer, or visualization exercises.

• **Tip**: Dedicate specific times each day or week to use your sacred space. Even just 10 minutes of stillness or focused intention can create powerful shifts.

• **Benefit**: Regular rituals keep your sacred space energetically active and aligned with your desires, helping you maintain focus and clarity in your healing or manifestation work (The Journal of Positive Psychology, 2019).

7. Use Sacred Sound

Incorporating sound into your sacred space can elevate its healing energy. Music, chanting, or the use of sound healing tools like tuning forks or singing bowls helps to create a vibrational frequency that enhances your intentions.

• **Practice**: Play calming music, mantras, or healing frequencies (such as 528 Hz) to help set the tone for your time in your sacred space.

• **Benefit**: Sound therapy has been shown to reduce stress, improve mood, and enhance clarity, making it a powerful tool for manifestation and healing (ScienceDirect, 2020).

8. Stay Open to the Process

As you engage with your sacred space, stay open to how it evolves. Your needs and goals may change over time, and your space should reflect that growth. Regularly revisit your intentions and adjust the items or rituals to keep your energy aligned with your current path.

• **Tip**: Periodically cleanse the space again and re-evaluate your intentions. If something no longer serves your growth, release it.

• **Benefit**: Regular updates keep the space dynamic and ensure it continues to be a supportive environment for your healing and manifestation journey (Psychology Today, 2020).

Creating a sacred space for healing and manifestation is not just about the physical environment; it's about consciously cultivating energy and intention that supports your personal growth. By following these steps and maintaining mindfulness, you can turn any space into a powerful tool for transformation and alignment with your highest self.

Designing spaces for mindfulness practices like yoga or prayer.

Designing spaces for mindfulness practices like yoga or prayer is about creating an environment that fosters relaxation, focus, and spiritual connection. Such spaces should encourage calm, promote mental clarity, and support physical comfort. Here's a guide to creating mindful spaces that cater to activities like yoga, meditation, prayer, or other spiritual practices.

1. Choose a Quiet, Secluded Location

The first step is selecting a space free from distractions and noise. A dedicated area that can be reserved solely for mindfulness practices is ideal, whether it's a room, corner, or even a spot in your garden. This will allow you to consistently return to this space for calmness and focus.

• **Tip**: Choose a spot with minimal foot traffic, such as a corner of a room, a balcony, or a quiet nook, so you can create an atmosphere of solitude.

• **Benefit**: A dedicated, peaceful space enhances the sense of sacredness and helps mentally prepare you for mindfulness activities (American Psychological Association, 2020).

2. Focus on Natural Light and Ventilation

Lighting is crucial for creating a serene environment. Natural light is ideal as it boosts mood and energy levels, which is especially beneficial for yoga and prayer. If natural light isn't available, consider using soft, warm artificial lighting, such as salt lamps or diffused light.

• **Tip**: Open windows to let in fresh air when possible, or incorporate plants to improve air quality and connection to nature.

• **Benefit**: Natural light helps regulate circadian rhythms, making the space conducive to rest, reflection, and focus (Harvard Health Publishing, 2020).

3. Keep the Space Clean and Clutter-Free

A cluttered space can distract and hinder your mindfulness practices. Keeping your environment clean, organized, and minimalist supports clarity of mind and a sense of calm. It's important to remove any non-essential items or distractions, leaving only those objects that promote peace.

• **Practice**: Use simple, functional storage solutions to keep unnecessary items out of sight, creating a clean, open space.

• **Benefit**: A clean environment has been shown to reduce stress and improve mental clarity, which enhances mindfulness practices (Psychology Today, 2019).

4. Use Natural Elements to Connect with the Earth

Incorporating natural elements, such as plants, wood, or stones, can help ground you during mindfulness practices. For yoga or prayer, these materials symbolize the connection between your body, mind, and the earth, enhancing feelings of stability and presence.

• **Tip**: Add plants like peace lilies or lavender for a calming effect, or use a wooden yoga block or cushion for added comfort and grounding.

• **Benefit**: Studies show that connecting with nature, even through small elements in your environment, can reduce stress and improve overall well-being (National Geographic, 2020).

5. Create Comfort with Soft Fabrics and Pillows

Comfort is key for physical practices like yoga or seated prayer. Use soft mats, pillows, cushions, or blankets to support your body during meditation or practice. A comfortable space encourages prolonged focus and relaxation without physical discomfort.

• **Practice**: Use cushions or bolsters for seated meditation or yoga poses. A yoga mat with enough padding will support your joints during practice.

• **Benefit**: Comfort enhances physical relaxation, which supports mental relaxation and helps focus your mind on the practice (MindBodyGreen, 2020).

6. Choose Calming Colors and Textures

Color plays a big role in setting the tone of a space. For a mindfulness area, focus on soft, calming colors such as shades of blue, green, beige, or lavender, which are known to have soothing effects. Textures should be soft and inviting to create a tactile sense of comfort.

• **Tip**: Use neutral tones for the walls, and add textured items like woven rugs or soft curtains to promote a calm atmosphere.

• **Benefit**: Research shows that colors like blue and green are associated with calming effects, reducing stress and promoting focus (Journal of Environmental Psychology, 2016).

7. Use Sound to Create a Peaceful Atmosphere

Sound is a powerful tool for enhancing mindfulness practices. Gentle music, chanting, singing bowls, or nature sounds (like birdsong or flowing water) can help create an atmosphere conducive to yoga, prayer, or meditation.

• **Practice**: Consider using a sound machine or a playlist of calming music, such as Tibetan singing bowls, to enhance the atmosphere.

• **Benefit**: Sound therapy has been linked to improved mood, reduced anxiety, and enhanced focus (The Journal of Alternative and Complementary Medicine, 2013).

8. Incorporate Meaningful Rituals and Symbols

Your sacred space can be further enriched with symbols or objects that represent your intentions, whether it's for meditation, yoga, or prayer. For example, a candle can symbolize the light of awareness, or a statue might represent a guiding figure.

• **Tip**: Incorporate items that hold personal significance, such as prayer beads, crystals, or sacred texts, depending on your spiritual or mindfulness practices.

• **Benefit**: Objects that symbolize your spiritual or mindfulness goals help anchor you to your intentions and support a deeper connection during your practices (Psychology Today, 2020).

9. Maintain Flexibility for Different Practices

Mindfulness can take many forms, and so should your space. Make your environment adaptable to suit a variety of practices, whether it's for yoga poses, seated meditation, or prayer.

• **Tip**: Use a low shelf or storage for yoga props like blocks, straps, and cushions. A small, portable altar can be moved or adjusted depending on the practice.

• **Benefit**: Flexibility allows your sacred space to evolve with your needs, ensuring that it always serves your mindfulness or spiritual journey (The Journal of Positive Psychology, 2019).

10. Add Personal Touches

Lastly, make the space your own by incorporating items that make you feel connected to your practice and yourself. Personal touches could include artwork, photographs, or items that bring peace and inspiration.

• **Tip**: Include visual elements like inspiring artwork or hand-written affirmations that align with your intentions.

• **Benefit**: Personalizing your space helps cultivate a deeper emotional connection to your practice and encourages consistency and focus.

By thoughtfully designing a space that prioritizes comfort, calm, and connection, you can create an environment that supports your mindfulness practices, helping you deepen your practice and enhance your overall well-being. Whether you're doing yoga, prayer, or meditation, your space becomes an essential partner in your journey of inner peace and spiritual growth.

Using affirmations and vision boards to reinforce positivity.

Using **affirmations** and **vision boards** is a powerful way to reinforce positivity and manifest your goals. Both tools help to focus the mind, align energy, and build a mindset of success. Here's how they work individually and together to create a positive shift in your life:

1. Affirmations: Power of Positive Thinking

Affirmations are short, positive statements that you repeat to yourself, often with the intent to challenge negative thoughts or reinforce empowering beliefs. They help create a positive mental environment by counteracting limiting beliefs, and with consistency, can lead to tangible changes in how you view yourself and your capabilities.

• **How it Works**: Repeating affirmations helps to reprogram the subconscious mind by shifting negative thought patterns into positive ones. This is based on the concept of **neuroplasticity**, which shows that the brain can change and form new neural connections over time through repeated thought and practice (Psychology Today, 2020).

• **Examples**: "I am worthy of love and success," or "I attract positivity and abundance into my life."

Benefits of Affirmations:

• **Mental Reprogramming**: Affirmations can reshape self-perception and help individuals overcome doubts or insecurities (Harvard Health Publishing, 2019).

• **Increased Self-Confidence**: Research indicates that regular affirmation practice can boost confidence and resilience, particularly in challenging situations (Journal of Social and Clinical Psychology, 2018).

How to Use Affirmations:

• **Consistency**: Choose a set of affirmations that resonate with you and repeat them daily, preferably in the morning or before going to sleep.

• **Emotional Alignment**: It's important to not only say the affirmation but also feel it—this emotional connection amplifies its power.

2. Vision Boards: Visualizing Success

A vision board is a tool for visualization, where you create a collage of images, words, and symbols that represent your goals, dreams, and aspirations. It serves as a physical reminder of what you're working toward and can help clarify your intentions.

• **How it Works**: The practice of creating a vision board is rooted in the **Law of Attraction**, which suggests that focusing on positive thoughts and images helps attract those things into your life (The Secret, 2006). By visualizing your goals daily, you reinforce your focus and increase your motivation to take actions aligned with your desires.

Benefits of Vision Boards:

• **Focus and Motivation**: Research suggests that visualizing success can increase the likelihood of achieving your goals. Vision boards keep your desires in the forefront of your mind, motivating you to take steps toward them (Harvard Business Review, 2015).

• **Connection to Emotions**: Vision boards create an emotional connection to your dreams, making them feel more attainable. The process of creating a vision board engages your creativity and aligns your emotions with your goals, which helps build confidence (Psychology Today, 2018).

How to Use Vision Boards:

• **Clarity**: Start by defining clear, specific goals for your life. These can be personal, professional, or spiritual.

• **Materialization**: Once you know your goals, gather magazines, printouts, or even digital images that represent them, and arrange them on a board. Place the vision board somewhere you'll see it regularly, like by your desk or next to your bed.

• **Affirmations with Vision Boards**: Pair your vision board with affirmations that reinforce your goals. For example, if you have a vision of financial abundance, you might use an affirmation like, "I am open to receiving wealth and success."

Combining Affirmations and Vision Boards

Using **both** affirmations and vision boards together is an even more potent way to reinforce positivity. Affirmations provide the verbal reinforcement and inner mindset shift, while vision boards keep you visually focused on your goals.

• **Daily Practice**: Begin your day by reviewing your vision board and then recite affirmations that align with what you want to manifest. This combination of visual and verbal practices helps to solidify your intention and raise your vibrational energy (Greater Good Science Center, 2019).

• **Manifestation Synergy**: Vision boards show you where you're headed, while affirmations ensure you're moving forward with the right mindset and energy. This synergy can dramatically enhance your ability to manifest your goals.

Scientific Support

Both affirmations and vision boards have psychological backing. Research has found that focusing on positive images and thoughts can help rewire the brain, increase resilience, and boost motivation. Regular visualization and positive affirmations not only enhance emotional well-being but can also improve your chances of success by conditioning your brain to look for opportunities that align with your desires.

Affirmations and vision boards are two complementary tools that, when used together, can create a powerful system of manifestation. By reinforcing positive thought patterns and keeping your goals at the forefront of your mind, you can shift your energy and align your actions with your desires. Whether you're striving for personal growth, career success, or emotional healing, these tools can support you in achieving your aspirations.

Chapter 8

Cultural and Spiritual Perspectives

Affirmations and vision boards are tools that are embraced across various **cultural** and **spiritual** traditions, each with its own interpretation of how these practices can support personal transformation, growth, and manifestation. While modern uses often draw from the **Law of Attraction** and personal development methods, these practices also have deep historical roots in numerous belief systems.

1. Affirmations in Cultural and Spiritual Contexts

Hinduism and Buddhism

In both **Hinduism** and **Buddhism**, the practice of **mantras** (which are similar to affirmations) has been used for thousands of years. A mantra is a word, sound, or phrase that is repeated, often during meditation, to focus the mind and invoke spiritual power. One of the most famous mantras is **"Om"**, considered to be the sound of the universe itself.

• **Hinduism**: In the tradition of **yoga**, affirmations are used to purify the mind and emotions. Repeating positive statements is believed to align the individual with divine consciousness and reduce mental clutter.

• **Buddhism**: The use of **mantras** in Tibetan Buddhism, such as "Om Mani Padme Hum," is thought to bring about spiritual enlightenment and a peaceful state of mind, as well as healing.

These practices highlight how affirmations, in the form of repeated sounds or phrases, are viewed not only as a tool for mental health but as a means of spiritual connection to something greater than the self (Eckhart Tolle, *The Power of Now*).

Native American Traditions

In many **Native American** cultures, affirmations are part of ceremonial practices. They may be used in rituals to invite abundance, healing, or protection, often through songs, prayers, or spoken words to the spirits. In these communities, affirmations are deeply connected to the elements of nature, acknowledging the interconnectedness of all things.

2. Vision Boards in Cultural and Spiritual Contexts

Ancient Egyptian and Greek Influence

The practice of visualizing one's goals and aspirations has roots that can be traced back to ancient civilizations. In **Ancient Egypt**, the concept of **"visualization"** was applied in religious and spiritual rituals, where the people would create symbols and representations of what they desired to manifest. The Egyptian practice of using **hieroglyphs** to symbolize divine intervention, protection, and prosperity aligns with the concept of vision boards—creating a symbolic representation of one's goals.

In **Ancient Greece**, the practice of **visualization** is attributed to philosophers like **Plato** and **Aristotle**, who discussed the idea of mental imagery and how it could lead to personal improvement and alignment with one's higher purpose.

Chinese Philosophy: The Law of Attraction

In **Chinese philosophy**, particularly through the lens of **Feng Shui**, there is an emphasis on aligning one's environment with personal and spiritual goals. This ancient practice stresses the importance of harmonious surroundings to attract positive energy. In modern interpretations, vision boards are seen as a contemporary evolution of this concept, where an individual uses visual cues to direct the flow of **Chi** (life energy) toward specific intentions.

• **Feng Shui** principles often suggest creating a **vision board** or similar representation of one's goals to ensure that the physical space aligns with the desired energies, helping to manifest success and harmony in one's life.

3. Affirmations and Vision Boards in Contemporary Spiritual Practices

While affirmations and vision boards are ancient practices, they have seen a resurgence in the **New Age** movement and **self-help** philosophies. Influenced by **The Secret** (Rhonda Byrne, 2006), these tools are often used together to create a powerful, focused, and intentional practice of manifestation.

In these contexts, affirmations are seen as a mental tool to create a mindset of abundance and self-worth, while vision boards serve as a physical representation of one's desires. Both tools are thought to help individuals tap into a universal energy (sometimes referred to as **source energy**) that aligns their desires with their actions.

• **New Age**: Practitioners believe that vision boards and affirmations help to **manifest desires** by focusing on what is desired and actively working to align one's thoughts, emotions, and energy with that vision.

Conclusion

From ancient spiritual traditions to modern-day practices, both **affirmations** and **vision boards** have deep cultural and spiritual roots. Whether through the use of mantras in Hinduism and Buddhism, the visualization techniques of Ancient Greece, or the environmental harmony practices of Feng Shui, these tools have always been linked to creating alignment between mind, body, and spirit. In today's world, they are widely used for personal development and goal setting, reinforcing the importance of aligning your thoughts and intentions with your desires in order to manifest positive changes in your life.

How various traditions (Feng Shui, Native American practices, etc.) approach cleansing and balance.

Different cultural and spiritual traditions have distinct methods for achieving cleansing and balance, often focused on restoring harmony between individuals, their environments, and the energies around them. These practices use a combination of rituals, symbolism, and tools to clear negative influences and create positive flow. Below are some prominent traditions, such as **Feng Shui**, **Native American practices**, and others, that offer diverse approaches to cleansing and balance.

1. Feng Shui: Clearing Negative Energy in the Environment

Feng Shui, the ancient Chinese practice, focuses on harmonizing the energy (Chi) within a living space to promote balance, prosperity, and well-being. **Cleansing** in Feng Shui typically involves the removal of energy blockages and the reorganization of physical spaces to enhance the flow of Chi.

• **Methods**: Feng Shui practitioners often recommend **space clearing** rituals that include:

○ **Burning incense or sage** to purify the air.

○ **Using mirrors** to reflect negative energy out of the space.

○ **Decluttering** and organizing to allow for the free flow of Chi.

○ **Placement of objects** such as plants, water fountains, and crystals to invite positive energy.

• **Balance**: Feng Shui principles emphasize the **Yin-Yang** balance (the duality of opposing energies) and the **Five Elements** (Wood, Fire, Earth, Metal, Water) to create harmony in a space. Proper placement of furniture, objects, and even colors can influence emotional and physical well-being.

Sources:

• **The Art of Feng Shui** (Marie Kondo, 2020)

• **Feng Shui for Dummies** (Stephen Skinner, 2011)

2. Native American Practices: Purification and Spiritual Cleansing

Native American spiritual practices often include purification rituals designed to cleanse both the body and the spirit. These rituals are performed to maintain balance and health within individuals and their communities.

• **Methods**:

○ **Sweat Lodge Ceremonies**: These rituals involve spending time in a small, enclosed space (often made of willow branches and covered with blankets) and sweating as a means of physical and spiritual purification. It is believed that the heat, combined with chanting and prayer, helps release negative emotions and energy.

○ **Smudging with Sage or Cedar**: **Smudging**, or the burning of sacred herbs like **white sage** or **cedar**, is a practice of purifying spaces, objects, and people. The smoke is believed to clear negative energy and create spiritual protection.

○ **Drumming and Dancing**: These are used to bring the mind and body into harmony with the natural world, often as part of a ceremony or celebration. Rhythmic drumming is thought to restore balance and connection with ancestral spirits.

• **Balance**: Native American traditions view balance as a relationship with nature, the earth, and the spirits. The goal is to restore **harmony** within the self and in relation to the universe, emphasizing respect for all living beings and natural cycles.

Sources:

• **The Sacred Pipe** (Joseph E. Brown, 1953)

• **Smudging and Blessings** (Sonja Grace, 2016)

3. Shamanic Practices: Energy Healing and Cleansing

Shamanic traditions, found in various indigenous cultures worldwide (such as the **Siberian**, **Amazonian**, and **North American** traditions), often involve rituals to cleanse the spirit, mind, and environment of negative energies.

• **Methods**:

○ **Soul Retrieval**: Shamans believe that negative experiences or trauma can cause parts of the soul to become fragmented. Soul retrieval ceremonies are conducted to recover these lost soul fragments and restore balance.

○ **Energy Cleansing**: Shamans use tools like **feathers**, **drums**, and **rattles** to clear negative energies from a person or space. Sacred herbs like **sage**, **sweetgrass**, and **palo santo** are burned, and sacred smoke is used to purify.

○ **Vision Quests**: A spiritual practice where individuals retreat into nature to fast and meditate, seeking visions or guidance from the spirit world for clarity and balance.

• **Balance**: Shamanic healing views balance as a spiritual journey of reconnecting with the earth and spirit, ensuring that individuals live in alignment with the natural world and cosmic forces.

Sources:

• **The Shaman's Path** (Michael Harner, 1990)

• **Shamanic Healing** (Karen Harrison, 2004)

4. Celtic Traditions: Purification through Nature and Rituals

Celtic traditions focus heavily on the natural world, believing that balance and healing can be achieved by reconnecting with the earth and the elements. The Celts practiced purification and cleansing rituals tied to the cycles of nature and the changing seasons.

• **Methods**:

○ **Burning Herbs and Incense**: **Celtic druids** used sacred herbs, such as **mugwort** and **lavender**, in cleansing rituals to purify spaces, individuals, and sacred sites.

○ **Water Cleansing**: Water has symbolic and literal healing properties. Rituals often involve immersing in or anointing with water from natural sources like rivers, streams, or sacred wells.

○ **Fire Rituals**: Fire is a powerful purifier in Celtic tradition, used in festivals like **Imbolc** or **Beltane** to cleanse and renew the energy of the community and individuals.

• **Balance**: The Celts understood balance through their **Triple Goddess** and **Gods of Nature**, symbolizing the interconnectedness of life, death, and rebirth. Seasonal festivals marked the balance between light and dark, life and death, helping individuals reconnect with their inner selves.

Sources:

• **The Celtic Spirit** (Carl McColman, 1999)

• **Celtic Wisdom and Healing** (Marion Woodman, 2001)

5. Ayurveda: Spiritual and Physical Cleansing

In **Ayurveda**, the ancient system of medicine from India, balance is achieved through harmony of the **doshas** (vital energies: Vata, Pitta, and Kapha). **Cleansing** is a crucial part of Ayurvedic health practices, as it removes toxins (called **Ama**) that block the flow of life energy.

• **Methods**:

o **Panchakarma**: A deep detoxification process that involves five main therapies, including **oil massages**, **herbal enemas**, and **nasal irrigation**, to clear the body of impurities and restore balance.

o **Pranayama (Breathwork)**: Breath control exercises that purify the mind and body, creating inner balance.

o **Herbal Cleansing**: Ayurvedic herbs such as **turmeric**, **ginger**, and **holy basil** are used to detoxify the body and mind, promote digestive health, and support emotional well-being.

• **Balance**: Ayurveda teaches that the goal of life is to live in harmony with **nature** and the **elements**, balancing body, mind, and spirit through diet, lifestyle, and rituals.

Sources:

• **The Ayurvedic Cookbook** (Amadea Morningstar, 1995)

• **Ayurveda: The Science of Self-Healing** (Vasant Lad, 1984)

Different traditions approach the concepts of cleansing and balance through their unique cultural and spiritual lenses, but they all share a common goal: to remove negative influences, restore harmony, and promote well-being. Whether through **Feng Shui's** focus on the environment, **Native American smudging rituals**, or **Ayurvedic detox** practices, these traditions demonstrate the deep connection between the mind, body, and spirit with the natural world and the energies around us.

Honoring the origins of cleansing practices respectfully.

Honoring the origins of cleansing practices is essential for respecting cultural and spiritual traditions while integrating their wisdom into modern life. Many cleansing rituals, whether for homes, individuals, or communities, have deep spiritual and cultural significance. Acknowledging this history and practicing these rituals with respect involves understanding the origins, meanings, and contexts in which they developed.

1. Respect for Sacredness

Many cleansing practices, like smudging with **sage** or **palo santo**, have sacred meanings in the **Native American** and **South American** indigenous cultures. These rituals are not just about clearing space, but also about connecting with spiritual realms, honoring ancestors, and fostering protection. For example, **sage smudging** is considered a prayer or offering, where the smoke carries intentions for healing and balance. To honor these practices respectfully, it's crucial to recognize the **spiritual** and **cultural significance** of the materials used.

Sources:

• **Smudging and Blessings** (Sonja Grace, 2016)

• **Sacred Smoke** (Diana P. Ault, 2007)

How to Honor:

• **Learn the History**: Before adopting any ritual, take time to understand its roots and the cultures from which it originates. This includes reading about the traditions and practices surrounding these rituals.

• **Proper Usage**: Use sacred materials like **sage** or **palo santo** with respect. Many indigenous groups consider these plants sacred, and their harvesting is often tied to specific rituals. Sourcing them responsibly and in consultation with knowledgeable community members helps honor their significance.

2. The Role of Intention

In **shamanic** traditions, cleansing rituals are not just about physical purification but also about the **intention** behind the action. Shamans and spiritual healers emphasize that the true power of a ritual lies in the energy, prayers, and emotions of the person performing the cleansing. The practice is believed to connect the individual to the spiritual realms, ancestors, and the **earth's energies**.

How to Honor:

• **Approach with Respect and Reverence**: Understand that the intention behind the ritual is just as important as the action. Shamans, for example, might purify spaces or people through rituals performed with deep respect and reverence for the spirits and ancestors involved.

Sources:

• **The Shamanic Path** (Michael Harner, 1990)

• **Shamanic Healing** (Karen Harrison, 2004)

3. Understanding the Cultural Context

When adopting **Feng Shui** principles, which come from **Chinese** philosophy, it's important to recognize that these practices emerged from a deep understanding of **natural forces** and **life energy** (Chi). Feng Shui is not just about creating aesthetically pleasing spaces—it's about aligning one's environment with cosmic energies to promote well-being. These practices are intricately linked to centuries of tradition, cosmology, and even **Confucian philosophy**.

How to Honor:

• **Learn the Cultural Significance**: Before implementing Feng Shui in your life, learn about its foundational philosophy, which emphasizes harmony with the universe. Practitioners often study Feng Shui for years to understand the nuances of these teachings.

• **Consult with a Practitioner**: To honor the origins of Feng Shui, consider consulting with a certified Feng Shui consultant or expert, especially if you wish to implement specific remedies in your home or workspace.

Sources:

- **The Art of Feng Shui** (Marie Kondo, 2020)

- **Feng Shui for Dummies** (Stephen Skinner, 2011)

4. Acknowledging the Role of Nature in Cleansing

In **Celtic** and other nature-based traditions, cleansing rituals often include elements like **water, fire,** and **herbs**—all of which are tied to the **natural world**. These traditions value the **cycles of nature**, viewing cleansing as a return to harmony with the environment. For example, **water rituals** in Celtic culture are used to purify and cleanse, reflecting an understanding of nature's flow.

How to Honor:

- **Use Natural Elements Mindfully**: Many Celtic rituals involve using natural elements in their purest form, such as **spring water** or **sacred herbs**. Be sure to source these items responsibly and sustainably, recognizing the sacredness of the earth's gifts.

- **Understand the Ecological Impact**: For example, with practices involving **herbal cleansing**, it's important to be mindful of over-harvesting and the ecological sustainability of the plants being used.

Sources:

- **The Celtic Spirit** (Carl McColman, 1999)

- **Celtic Wisdom and Healing** (Marion Woodman, 2001)

5. Modern Adaptations with Sensitivity

In modern contexts, many people use elements of these traditional practices to promote wellness or spiritual growth. While it's fine to incorporate these practices into your life, it's important to do so with sensitivity to the origins and cultural significance of each practice. For example, using **sage** for cleansing in a **New Age** context should still be done with the understanding that for many, **sage** is sacred and used for specific ceremonial purposes.

How to Honor:

• **Mindful Integration**: If you are adopting these practices for personal use, do so with mindfulness and respect. Acknowledge the cultural and spiritual meanings behind each ritual and make an effort to honor its sacredness.

• **Support Indigenous Communities**: Whenever possible, purchase cleansing tools like sage, cedar, or palo

Chapter 9

Sustaining a High-Vibration Lifestyle

Sustaining a high-vibration lifestyle is about maintaining a state of mental, emotional, and physical well-being that aligns with positive energy, vitality, and harmony. The idea is to create a life where your actions, thoughts, and environments resonate with the highest possible frequency, leading to greater joy, health, and fulfillment. This concept comes from both modern wellness practices and spiritual traditions, where high vibration is synonymous with being aligned to love, peace, and abundance.

Here are some key principles for sustaining a high-vibration lifestyle:

1. Nurturing Positive Thoughts and Emotions

High-vibration living starts with cultivating positive mental and emotional states. Your thoughts and emotions can significantly influence your energy frequency. Practices such as **affirmations**, **gratitude**, and **self-love** are tools that help maintain a positive mindset.

- **Affirmations**: These are positive statements that replace negative self-talk and help reprogram your mind. Studies show that repeating affirmations can improve self-esteem and overall mental health (see *Psychology Today* for details on their effectiveness).

- **Gratitude**: Gratitude journaling has been shown to boost happiness and improve emotional resilience. A study published in *The Journal of Positive Psychology* found that people who practiced gratitude regularly experienced more positive emotions, better sleep, and increased well-being.

- **Emotional Awareness**: Learning to process emotions rather than suppress them is also key to maintaining balance. Mindfulness and emotional regulation techniques can help avoid emotional extremes and maintain high vibration.

Sources:

- *Psychology Today* on affirmations

- *The Journal of Positive Psychology* on gratitude and well-being

2. Healthy Lifestyle Choices

Your body is an important aspect of your energy system. Maintaining physical health through nutrition, exercise, and sleep helps sustain a high-vibration lifestyle.

- **Nutrition**: Eating a clean, nutrient-rich diet, particularly foods that are **plant-based** or full of whole foods, supports energy levels and overall well-being. Avoiding processed foods, sugar, and excessive alcohol helps prevent the body from being bogged down by low-frequency foods.

- **Exercise**: Physical activity, especially practices like **yoga, tai chi**, or **walking in nature**, helps maintain energy flow. Regular exercise boosts the body's production of endorphins and improves circulation, which contributes to a more vibrant energy field.

• **Sleep**: Good quality sleep is crucial. It allows the body to heal and regenerate, helping to maintain both physical and emotional balance.

Sources:

• *Harvard Health* on the benefits of exercise

• *The Sleep Foundation* on sleep's impact on health

3. Cleanse and Purify Your Environment

The energy in your physical environment plays a significant role in your vibration. Cleansing your space from negative energy helps to create a more harmonious and high-vibration setting.

• **Decluttering**: A cluttered space often reflects mental clutter. A minimalist or organized space promotes clarity and peace of mind. Studies in psychology have shown that decluttering can reduce stress and improve concentration (*The Personality and Social Psychology Bulletin*).

• **Cleansing Rituals**: Smudging with sage, using crystals, or burning candles are traditional methods used to clear negative energy from a space. Practices like **Feng Shui** emphasize the importance of arranging your environment to ensure the optimal flow of energy.

• **Plants and Crystals**: Adding plants and healing crystals to your environment not only beautifies a space but also promotes a positive atmosphere. Plants release oxygen and purify the air, while crystals like **amethyst**, **clear quartz**, and **rose quartz** are thought to harmonize energy.

Sources:

• *The Personality and Social Psychology Bulletin* on clutter and stress

• *The Feng Shui Bible* by Simon Brown on energy flow in spaces

4. Connecting with Nature

Spending time in nature is one of the simplest and most effective ways to raise your vibration. Nature is inherently high-vibrational, and being outdoors helps reset your energy.

• **Forest Bathing**: Inspired by Japanese **Shinrin-yoku**, forest bathing is the practice of immersing yourself in nature to reduce stress and increase feelings of well-being. Research has shown that spending time in nature lowers cortisol levels, which reduces stress.

• **Water**: Water is considered one of the highest vibrational elements. Swimming, walking by a lake or beach, or even just drinking water can help recharge your energy.

Sources:

• *Shinrin-Yoku: The Art and Science of Forest Bathing* by Dr. Qing Li

• Studies on the benefits of water exposure from *The Environmental Health Perspectives Journal*

5. Mindful Practices and Meditation

Mindfulness, meditation, and breathwork are powerful tools for raising and sustaining your energy. They help you stay present, calm your nervous system, and cultivate inner peace.

• **Meditation**: Practicing daily meditation can dramatically improve your ability to stay connected to your inner self and raise your energy levels. Meditation is shown to help balance brain-waves, promote relaxation, and reduce emotional reactivity.

• **Breathwork**: Techniques such as **pranayama** or **box breathing** can help you clear emotional blockages, calm anxiety, and increase overall energy flow.

Sources:

• *Mindfulness-Based Stress Reduction* (MBSR) by Dr. Jon Kabat-Zinn

• Research on meditation benefits from *Harvard Medical School*

6. Surround Yourself with Positive Influences

The people you interact with and the media you consume play a significant role in your energy. Surrounding yourself with positive, supportive people and uplifting content helps keep your vibration high.

• **Positive Relationships**: Cultivating friendships with people who support your well-being and share your values can significantly boost your energy.

• **Limiting Negative Input**: Whether it's the news, social media, or negative conversations, limiting exposure to negativity helps protect your energy.

Sources:

• *The Power of Now* by Eckhart Tolle on the influence of relationships on energy

• *The Social Animal* by Elliot Aronson on social influence and emotional energy

7. Practicing Gratitude and Service

Maintaining a high vibration involves aligning your actions with love, compassion, and abundance. Practicing **gratitude** and **acts of service** can elevate your energy by focusing on giving and appreciating life.

• **Gratitude**: As mentioned, regular gratitude practices (journaling, verbalizing, or simply reflecting on things you're thankful for) can shift your focus from lack to abundance.

• **Service**: Acts of kindness and service to others not only improve their energy but also increase your sense of purpose and fulfillment.

Sources:

• *The Gratitude Diaries* by Janice Kaplan

• *The Art of Happiness* by Dalai Lama and Howard Cutler on the joy

Tips for maintaining positivity even in challenging environments.

Maintaining positivity in challenging environments can be difficult, but it is possible with consistent practices and mindset shifts. Here are some key strategies to help you stay positive even in tough circumstances:

1. Reframe Your Perspective

In challenging environments, it's easy to focus on the negativity around you. Reframing your thoughts involves shifting your focus from what you can't control to what you can.

• **Practice Gratitude**: Even in tough situations, finding small things to be grateful for can help shift your mindset. Studies show that gratitude can improve mental health and resilience by fostering a sense of appreciation and balance (*The Journal of Positive Psychology*).

• **Look for Learning Opportunities**: Instead of seeing challenges as setbacks, try to view them as opportunities for personal growth. Reframing difficulties as chances to develop resilience or new skills can reduce stress and increase optimism.

Sources: *The Journal of Positive Psychology* on gratitude and well-being, *The Power of Now* by Eckhart Tolle on reframing challenges.

2. Focus on What You Can Control

In environments where many factors are beyond your control, it's essential to focus on what is within your power.

• **Self-Care**: Focusing on daily self-care routines, such as exercise, nutrition, and relaxation, can help you feel grounded and in control. Research shows that self-care practices are effective in combating stress and improving overall well-being (*American Psychological Association*).

• **Boundaries**: Set healthy boundaries with people and situations that drain your energy. Learning to say "no" or distancing yourself from negative influences can preserve your peace and emotional stability.

Sources: *American Psychological Association* on self-care, *Boundaries* by Dr. Henry Cloud on emotional self-preservation.

3. Practice Mindfulness

Mindfulness is the practice of staying present and aware without judgment. It helps in managing stress and maintaining a positive mindset, especially in difficult situations.

- **Mindful Breathing**: Focusing on your breath can instantly calm your nervous system, helping you stay centered and less reactive. Techniques like **deep belly breathing** or **box breathing** can reduce anxiety and improve emotional regulation.

- **Meditation**: Regular mindfulness meditation can increase your ability to stay calm in challenging environments. Research from *Harvard Health* suggests that mindfulness practices reduce the impact of stress and improve emotional resilience.

Sources: *Harvard Health* on mindfulness meditation, *Mindfulness-Based Stress Reduction* by Dr. Jon Kabat-Zinn.

4. Engage in Acts of Kindness

Focusing on helping others, even in small ways, can boost your own mood and sense of positivity. Helping others fosters a sense of purpose and connection, which enhances well-being.

- **Volunteer or Offer Support**: Acts of service, such as volunteering or even offering a kind word to someone else, can create a ripple effect of positivity, lifting both your mood and those around you.

- **Random Acts of Kindness**: Even small, spontaneous acts of kindness (like complimenting a stranger or helping someone with a task) have been shown to increase happiness and reduce feelings of stress.

Sources: *The Art of Happiness* by Dalai Lama, *The Random Acts of Kindness* Foundation on the psychological benefits of kindness.

5. Limit Negative Exposure

In a challenging environment, it's easy to be overwhelmed by negativity, whether it comes from media, social interactions, or the workplace. Limiting exposure to negativity helps maintain a positive outlook.

• **Curate Your Media Consumption**: Avoid overconsumption of negative news or social media. Research shows that constant exposure to negative content can lead to anxiety and depression (*The American Journal of Epidemiology*).

• **Create a Positive Environment**: Surround yourself with positive people, uplifting music, or calming visuals. Even small adjustments to your environment, such as adding plants, art, or inspirational quotes, can help lift your energy.

Sources: *The American Journal of Epidemiology* on media consumption and mental health, *The Happiness Project* by Gretchen Rubin on creating a positive environment.

6. Seek Support and Connection

Connecting with others is a key factor in maintaining positivity. Even in difficult environments, having a support system can help you navigate stress and adversity.

• **Talk to Someone You Trust**: Sometimes, simply sharing your challenges with a trusted friend or therapist can provide relief. Research shows that social support is a key factor in resilience and mental health.

• **Join a Support Group**: Participating in groups, whether online or in-person, with people who share similar experiences or goals can help provide a sense of community and hope.

Sources: *Social Support and Mental Health* by Cohen and Wills, *The Gift of Therapy* by Irvin D. Yalom on the importance of social support.

7. Focus on the Bigger Picture

Sometimes, when you're in a difficult environment, it helps to remind yourself of the bigger picture. This means keeping your long-term goals, values, and sense of purpose in mind, rather than getting bogged down by temporary struggles.

• **Set Intentional Goals**: Reflecting on your bigger life goals and values helps align your actions with your highest aspirations. This keeps you motivated and focused on what truly matters.

• **Remember Your Purpose**: When life gets tough, reconnect with your sense of purpose or personal mission. Whether it's related to your work, family, or passions, having a sense of purpose can provide strength and clarity in challenging times.

Sources: *Start with Why* by Simon Sinek, *Man's Search for Meaning* by Viktor Frankl on purpose and resilience.

8. Stay Physically Active

Physical movement is not only good for your body but also supports your emotional and mental health.

• **Exercise**: Even light exercise like walking or stretching can boost endorphins and help counteract stress. Studies show that physical activity enhances mood and reduces anxiety (*The Mayo Clinic*).

• **Movement Breaks**: Take breaks to stretch or walk, especially in high-stress situations. This simple act can refresh your mind and body, making it easier to maintain a positive outlook.

Sources: *The Mayo Clinic* on exercise and mental health, *The Happiness Advantage* by Shawn Achor on physical activity and positivity.

By integrating these strategies into your daily life, you can maintain positivity, even in the most challenging environments. It's important to remember that these practices require time and consistency, but the benefits of cultivating a high-vibration mindset are immense—improved mental health, better relationships, and an overall greater sense of peace.

Building supportive relationships and letting go of toxic ones.

Building supportive relationships and letting go of toxic ones is a powerful step toward creating a more positive and balanced life. Positive relationships uplift us, provide emotional support, and help us grow, while toxic relationships can drain energy, cause emotional harm, and hinder our personal development. Here's how to foster supportive connections and let go of toxic ones:

1. Recognize the Signs of Supportive vs. Toxic Relationships

• **Supportive Relationships**: These relationships are characterized by mutual respect, trust, encouragement, and emotional safety. In these connections, both parties feel heard, valued, and nurtured.

• **Toxic Relationships**: Toxic relationships can be marked by manipulation, criticism, dishonesty, control, or emotional abuse. These relationships often cause feelings of anxiety, resentment, or self-doubt.

Sources:

• *Psychology Today* on supportive relationships and mental health

• *The Gift of Fear* by Gavin de Becker on recognizing toxic relationships

2. Cultivate Healthy Communication

Effective communication is the foundation of any strong relationship. In supportive relationships, both individuals are able to express their thoughts and feelings openly and respectfully, and they listen to each other's needs.

In contrast, toxic relationships often involve poor communication or manipulation, where one person's needs dominate or go unaddressed.

Tips:

• Practice active listening, where you focus fully on what the other person is saying, without judgment or interruption.

• Use "I" statements to express how you feel without blaming or accusing (e.g., "I feel upset when...").

Sources:

• *Nonviolent Communication* by Marshall Rosenberg

• *The 5 Love Languages* by Gary Chapman on communication in relationships

3. Set Healthy Boundaries

Boundaries are essential for maintaining a balanced relationship. They protect your emotional space, ensuring that you're not being taken advantage of or compromising your well-being.

In toxic relationships, boundaries are often ignored or violated, leading to feelings of depletion and resentment.

Tips:

• Be clear and assertive about your needs and limitations.

• Learn to say "no" without feeling guilty, especially when the other person's demands are unreasonable.

• Reinforce your boundaries consistently, without fear of retribution.

Sources:

• *Boundaries* by Dr. Henry Cloud and Dr. John Townsend

• *Radical Acceptance* by Tara Brach on emotional boundaries and self-care

4. Identify Toxic Patterns and Let Go

Letting go of toxic relationships requires awareness and courage. You may notice consistent patterns of behavior that harm you, such as emotional manipulation, deceit, or lack of respect.

Tips:

• **Trust your feelings**: If someone consistently makes you feel bad about yourself or causes you stress, it's important to trust your gut.

• **Distance yourself**: Gradually distancing yourself from toxic individuals can help you reclaim your energy and emotional health.

• **Seek professional support**: If you're struggling to let go, talking to a therapist can provide insight and guidance on navigating difficult relationships.

Sources:

• *The Drama of the Gifted Child* by Alice Miller on the psychology of toxic relationships

• *Psychology Today* article on toxic relationships and emotional health

5. Surround Yourself with Positive, Like-Minded People

To build a supportive network, actively seek out relationships with people who share your values, interests, and goals. Healthy friendships and relationships bring joy, confidence, and shared energy.

Tips:

• Participate in activities or groups that align with your values, such as volunteering, sports, or creative hobbies.

• Foster relationships based on mutual respect, where you both give and receive equally.

• Invest time in people who uplift you and avoid those who drain your energy.

Sources:

• *The Happiness Project* by Gretchen Rubin on building supportive communities

• *Daring Greatly* by Brené Brown on cultivating vulnerability and connection

6. Practice Forgiveness and Release Resentment

Letting go of toxic relationships doesn't always mean cutting someone out of your life completely—it can also mean forgiving past hurts and releasing the emotional grip that the relationship holds over you.

Tips:

• **Forgive yourself**: Often, we stay in toxic relationships because of guilt or fear of judgment. Self-forgiveness is the first step toward healing.

• **Let go of resentment**: Holding onto resentment only harms your mental health. Practice mindfulness or journaling to process negative emotions and release the past.

Sources:

• *The Gifts of Imperfection* by Brené Brown on letting go of past wounds

• *Radical Forgiveness* by Colin Tipping on healing through forgiveness

7. Commit to Continuous Self-Reflection

Regularly reflect on your relationships and the role you play in them. This self-awareness helps you maintain positive connections and address any unhealthy patterns you might be contributing to.

Tips:

• Set aside time to reflect on your interactions and whether your needs are being met in each relationship.

• If you notice unhealthy dynamics emerging, take proactive steps to address them, either through communication or boundary-setting.

Sources:

• *Emotional Intelligence* by Daniel Goleman on self-awareness and emotional health

• *The Four Agreements* by Don Miguel Ruiz on self-reflection and personal growth

8. Seek Support When Needed

Finally, don't hesitate to seek support when navigating difficult relationships. Having a therapist, coach, or trusted friend to confide in can provide clarity and emotional reinforcement.

Sources:

• *The Body Keeps the Score* by Bessel van der Kolk on trauma and emotional healing

• *Toxic Parents* by Susan Forward on overcoming the influence of toxic relationships

By recognizing the signs of supportive vs. toxic relationships, setting boundaries, and committing to self-care and reflection, you can create and maintain a network of relationships that enhance your well-being and allow you to thrive. Letting go of toxic people may feel difficult at first, but it's an essential step toward preserving your energy, peace, and overall happiness.

The End